Application Functionality
Complete Self-Assessment Guide

Table of Contents

About The Art of Service

The Art of Service, Business Process Architects since 2000, is dedicated to helping stakeholders achieve excellence.

Defining, designing, creating, and implementing a process to solve a stakeholders challenge or meet an objective is the most valuable role… In EVERY group, company, organization and department.

Unless you're talking a one-time, single-use project, there should be a process. Whether that process is managed and implemented by humans, AI, or a combination of the two, it needs to be designed by someone with a complex enough perspective to ask the right questions.

Someone capable of asking the right questions and step back and say, 'What are we really trying to accomplish here? And is there a different way to look at it?'

With The Art of Service's Standard Requirements Self-Assessments, we empower people who can do just that — whether their title is marketer, entrepreneur, manager, salesperson, consultant, Business Process Manager, executive assistant, IT Manager, CIO etc... —they are the people who rule the future. They are people who watch the process as it happens, and ask the right questions to make the process work better.

Contact us when you need any support with this Self-Assessment and any help with templates, blue-prints and examples of standard documents you might need:

http://theartofservice.com
service@theartofservice.com

Included Resources - how to access

Included with your purchase of the book is the Application

Functionality Self-Assessment Spreadsheet Dashboard which contains all questions and Self-Assessment areas and auto-generates insights, graphs, and project RACI planning - all with examples to get you started right away.

How? Simply send an email to
access@theartofservice.com
with this books' title in the subject to get the Application Functionality Self Assessment Tool right away.

You will receive the following contents with New and Updated specific criteria:

- The latest quick edition of the book in PDF

- The latest complete edition of the book in PDF, which criteria correspond to the criteria in...

- The Self-Assessment Excel Dashboard, and...

- Example pre-filled Self-Assessment Excel Dashboard to get familiar with results generation

- In-depth specific Checklists covering the topic

- Project management checklists and templates to assist with implementation

INCLUDES LIFETIME SELF ASSESSMENT UPDATES

Every self assessment comes with Lifetime Updates and Lifetime Free Updated Books. Lifetime Updates is an industry-first feature which allows you to receive verified self assessment updates, ensuring you always have the most accurate information at your fingertips.

Get it now- you will be glad you did - do it now, before you forget.

Send an email to **access@theartofservice.com** with this books' title in the subject to get the Application Functionality Self Assessment Tool right away.

Purpose of this Self-Assessment

This Self-Assessment has been developed to improve understanding of the requirements and elements of Application Functionality, based on best practices and standards in business process architecture, design and quality management.

It is designed to allow for a rapid Self-Assessment to determine how closely existing management practices and procedures correspond to the elements of the Self-Assessment.

The criteria of requirements and elements of Application Functionality have been rephrased in the format of a Self-Assessment questionnaire, with a seven-criterion scoring system, as explained in this document.

In this format, even with limited background knowledge of Application Functionality, a manager can quickly review existing operations to determine how they measure up to the standards. This in turn can serve as the starting point of a 'gap analysis' to identify management tools or system elements that might usefully be implemented in the organization to help improve overall performance.

How to use the Self-Assessment

On the following pages are a series of questions to identify to what extent your Application Functionality initiative is complete in comparison to the requirements set in standards.

To facilitate answering the questions, there is a space in front of each question to enter a score on a scale of '1' to '5'.

1 Strongly Disagree

2 Disagree

3 Neutral

4 Agree

5 Strongly Agree

Read the question and rate it with the following in front of mind:

'In my belief, the answer to this question is clearly defined'.

There are two ways in which you can choose to interpret this statement;
1. how aware are you that the answer to the question is clearly defined
2. for more in-depth analysis you can choose to gather evidence and confirm the answer to the question. This obviously will take more time, most Self-Assessment users opt for the first way to interpret the question and dig deeper later on based on the outcome of the overall Self-Assessment.

A score of '1' would mean that the answer is not clear at all, where a '5' would mean the answer is crystal clear and defined. Leave emtpy when the question is not applicable or you don't want to answer it, you can skip it without affecting your score. Write your score in the space provided.

After you have responded to all the appropriate statements in each section, compute your average score for that section, using the formula provided, and round to the nearest tenth. Then transfer to the corresponding spoke in the Application Functionality Scorecard on the second next page of the Self-Assessment.

Your completed Application Functionality Scorecard will give you a clear presentation of which Application Functionality areas need attention.

Application Functionality Scorecard Example

Example of how the finalized Scorecard can look like:

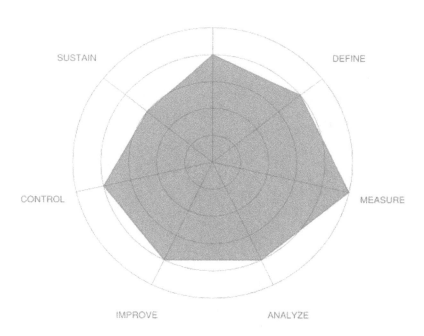

Application Functionality Scorecard

Your Scores:

BEGINNING OF THE SELF-ASSESSMENT:

CRITERION #1: RECOGNIZE

INTENT: Be aware of the need for change. Recognize that there is an unfavorable variation, problem or symptom.

In my belief, the answer to this question is clearly defined:

5 Strongly Agree

4 Agree

3 Neutral

2 Disagree

1 Strongly Disagree

1. What training and capacity building actions are needed to implement proposed reforms?
<--- Score

2. Does your organization need more application functionality education?
<--- Score

3. What vendors make products that address the

application functionality needs?
<--- Score

4. What extra resources will you need?
<--- Score

5. Where is training needed?
<--- Score

6. Do you need different information or graphics?
<--- Score

7. What resources or support might you need?
<--- Score

8. How do you identify the kinds of information that you will need?
<--- Score

9. Who defines the rules in relation to any given issue?
<--- Score

10. Are your goals realistic? Do you need to redefine your problem? Perhaps the problem has changed or maybe you have reached your goal and need to set a new one?
<--- Score

11. Are there application functionality problems defined?
<--- Score

12. Whom do you really need or want to serve?
<--- Score

13. How does it fit into your organizational needs and tasks?

<--- Score

14. How can auditing be a preventative security measure?

<--- Score

15. What are the minority interests and what amount of minority interests can be recognized?

<--- Score

16. Which issues are too important to ignore?

<--- Score

17. What prevents you from making the changes you know will make you a more effective application functionality leader?

<--- Score

18. What problems are you facing and how do you consider application functionality will circumvent those obstacles?

<--- Score

19. Do you recognize application functionality achievements?

<--- Score

20. What are the clients issues and concerns?

<--- Score

21. Is it clear when you think of the day ahead of you what activities and tasks you need to complete?

<--- Score

22. What are your needs in relation to application functionality skills, labor, equipment, and markets?

<--- Score

23. What would happen if application functionality weren't done?

<--- Score

24. What are the expected benefits of application functionality to the stakeholder?

<--- Score

25. Think about the people you identified for your application functionality project and the project responsibilities you would assign to them, what kind of training do you think they would need to perform these responsibilities effectively?

<--- Score

26. Can management personnel recognize the monetary benefit of application functionality?

<--- Score

27. How do you recognize an application functionality objection?

<--- Score

28. What information do users need?

<--- Score

29. Will new equipment/products be required to facilitate application functionality delivery, for example is new software needed?

<--- Score

30. When a application functionality manager recognizes a problem, what options are available?
<--- Score

31. Which information does the application functionality business case need to include?
<--- Score

32. Who needs to know about application functionality?
<--- Score

33. Are there any specific expectations or concerns about the application functionality team, application functionality itself?
<--- Score

34. Did you miss any major application functionality issues?
<--- Score

35. What is the recognized need?
<--- Score

36. For your application functionality project, identify and describe the business environment, is there more than one layer to the business environment?
<--- Score

37. Who needs to know?
<--- Score

38. Does application functionality create potential expectations in other areas that need to be recognized and considered?
<--- Score

39. Are problem definition and motivation clearly presented?
<--- Score

40. What application functionality problem should be solved?
<--- Score

41. Are you dealing with any of the same issues today as yesterday? What can you do about this?
<--- Score

42. What needs to be done?
<--- Score

43. What application functionality events should you attend?
<--- Score

44. What does application functionality success mean to the stakeholders?
<--- Score

45. Do you know what you need to know about application functionality?
<--- Score

46. What are the timeframes required to resolve each of the issues/problems?
<--- Score

47. What is the problem and/or vulnerability?
<--- Score

48. What application functionality coordination do

you need?
<--- Score

49. Is it needed?
<--- Score

50. Is the quality assurance team identified?
<--- Score

51. Looking at each person individually – does every one have the qualities which are needed to work in this group?
<--- Score

52. Are there regulatory / compliance issues?
<--- Score

53. Are employees recognized for desired behaviors?
<--- Score

54. Is the need for organizational change recognized?
<--- Score

55. Consider your own application functionality project, what types of organizational problems do you think might be causing or affecting your problem, based on the work done so far?
<--- Score

56. Are controls defined to recognize and contain problems?
<--- Score

57. What needs to stay?
<--- Score

58. Will application functionality deliverables need to be tested and, if so, by whom?
<--- Score

59. To what extent does each concerned units management team recognize application functionality as an effective investment?
<--- Score

60. How are training requirements identified?
<--- Score

61. How do you identify subcontractor relationships?
<--- Score

62. Why the need?
<--- Score

63. How much are sponsors, customers, partners, stakeholders involved in application functionality? In other words, what are the risks, if application functionality does not deliver successfully?
<--- Score

64. Have you identified your application functionality key performance indicators?
<--- Score

65. Who else hopes to benefit from it?
<--- Score

66. How do you recognize an objection?
<--- Score

67. How are you going to measure success?
<--- Score

68. What is the problem or issue?
<--- Score

69. Would you recognize a threat from the inside?
<--- Score

70. Will a response program recognize when a crisis occurs and provide some level of response?
<--- Score

71. What do you need to start doing?
<--- Score

72. Are there any revenue recognition issues?
<--- Score

73. Do you have/need 24-hour access to key personnel?
<--- Score

74. Why is this needed?
<--- Score

75. Who needs budgets?
<--- Score

76. Who should resolve the application functionality issues?
<--- Score

77. What are the stakeholder objectives to be achieved with application functionality?
<--- Score

78. Where do you need to exercise leadership?

<--- Score

79. What creative shifts do you need to take?
<--- Score

80. Do you need to avoid or amend any application functionality activities?
<--- Score

81. What do employees need in the short term?
<--- Score

82. As a sponsor, customer or management, how important is it to meet goals, objectives?
<--- Score

83. Who are your key stakeholders who need to sign off?
<--- Score

84. What should be considered when identifying available resources, constraints, and deadlines?
<--- Score

85. Will it solve real problems?
<--- Score

86. Are employees recognized or rewarded for performance that demonstrates the highest levels of integrity?
<--- Score

87. What is the smallest subset of the problem you can usefully solve?
<--- Score

88. Are losses recognized in a timely manner?
<--- Score

89. How are the application functionality's objectives aligned to the group's overall stakeholder strategy?
<--- Score

90. What activities does the governance board need to consider?
<--- Score

91. What is the application functionality problem definition? What do you need to resolve?
<--- Score

92. How do you take a forward-looking perspective in identifying application functionality research related to market response and models?
<--- Score

93. What application functionality capabilities do you need?
<--- Score

94. What is the extent or complexity of the application functionality problem?
<--- Score

95. What situation(s) led to this application functionality Self Assessment?
<--- Score

Add up total points for this section:
_ _ _ _ _ = Total points for this section

Divided by: _ _ _ _ _ _ (number of

statements answered) = _ _ _ _ _ _
Average score for this section

Transfer your score to the application
functionality Index at the beginning of
the Self-Assessment.

CRITERION #2: DEFINE:

INTENT: Formulate the stakeholder problem. Define the problem, needs and objectives.

In my belief, the answer to this question is clearly defined:

5 Strongly Agree

4 Agree

3 Neutral

2 Disagree

1 Strongly Disagree

1. What are the application functionality tasks and definitions?
<--- Score

2. How do you think the partners involved in application functionality would have defined success?
<--- Score

3. Does the team have regular meetings?
<--- Score

4. What customer feedback methods were used to solicit their input?
<--- Score

5. Is the work to date meeting requirements?
<--- Score

6. Is there any additional application functionality definition of success?
<--- Score

7. How was the 'as is' process map developed, reviewed, verified and validated?
<--- Score

8. How would you define application functionality leadership?
<--- Score

9. Has the direction changed at all during the course of application functionality? If so, when did it change and why?
<--- Score

10. Do you all define application functionality in the same way?
<--- Score

11. The political context: who holds power?
<--- Score

12. Is application functionality currently on schedule according to the plan?

<--- Score

13. What is the definition of application functionality excellence?
<--- Score

14. What would be the goal or target for a application functionality's improvement team?
<--- Score

15. What are the record-keeping requirements of application functionality activities?
<--- Score

16. What are the core elements of the application functionality business case?
<--- Score

17. What is the scope of application functionality?
<--- Score

18. How is the team tracking and documenting its work?
<--- Score

19. What are the Roles and Responsibilities for each team member and its leadership? Where is this documented?
<--- Score

20. How and when will the baselines be defined?
<--- Score

21. Is application functionality required?
<--- Score

22. Is application functionality linked to key stakeholder goals and objectives?
<--- Score

23. What key stakeholder process output measure(s) does application functionality leverage and how?
<--- Score

24. Is the application functionality scope manageable?
<--- Score

25. Is the scope of application functionality defined?
<--- Score

26. What happens if application functionality's scope changes?
<--- Score

27. What are the application functionality use cases?
<--- Score

28. What is the worst case scenario?
<--- Score

29. What sources do you use to gather information for a application functionality study?
<--- Score

30. Where can you gather more information?
<--- Score

31. Why are you doing application functionality and what is the scope?
<--- Score

32. Are the application functionality requirements complete?
<--- Score

33. Has/have the customer(s) been identified?
<--- Score

34. Is there a application functionality management charter, including stakeholder case, problem and goal statements, scope, milestones, roles and responsibilities, communication plan?
<--- Score

35. How do you build the right business case?
<--- Score

36. Is data collected and displayed to better understand customer(s) critical needs and requirements.
<--- Score

37. How do you manage unclear application functionality requirements?
<--- Score

38. What specifically is the problem? Where does it occur? When does it occur? What is its extent?
<--- Score

39. When is/was the application functionality start date?
<--- Score

40. How does the application functionality manager ensure against scope creep?
<--- Score

41. Who approved the application functionality scope?
<--- Score

42. What constraints exist that might impact the team?
<--- Score

43. Is scope creep really all bad news?
<--- Score

44. Is the team adequately staffed with the desired cross-functionality? If not, what additional resources are available to the team?
<--- Score

45. What application functionality requirements should be gathered?
<--- Score

46. Is there regularly 100% attendance at the team meetings? If not, have appointed substitutes attended to preserve cross-functionality and full representation?
<--- Score

47. What are the tasks and definitions?
<--- Score

48. Is the improvement team aware of the different versions of a process: what they think it is vs. what it actually is vs. what it should be vs. what it could be?
<--- Score

49. Do you have a application functionality success

story or case study ready to tell and share?
<--- Score

50. Are there different segments of customers?
<--- Score

51. Are task requirements clearly defined?
<--- Score

52. What critical content must be communicated –
who, what, when, where, and how?
<--- Score

53. What is the scope of the application functionality
work?
<--- Score

54. What are the rough order estimates on cost
savings/opportunities that application functionality
brings?
<--- Score

55. Are different versions of process maps needed to
account for the different types of inputs?
<--- Score

**56. Are the application functionality requirements
testable?**
<--- Score

57. Has a team charter been developed and
communicated?
<--- Score

58. What information do you gather?
<--- Score

59. What is in scope?
<--- Score

60. When are meeting minutes sent out? Who is on the distribution list?
<--- Score

61. Are roles and responsibilities formally defined?
<--- Score

62. What are (control) requirements for application functionality Information?
<--- Score

63. Are customer(s) identified and segmented according to their different needs and requirements?
<--- Score

64. How do you manage scope?
<--- Score

65. Are accountability and ownership for application functionality clearly defined?
<--- Score

66. Are there any constraints known that bear on the ability to perform application functionality work? How is the team addressing them?
<--- Score

67. What are the requirements for audit information?
<--- Score

68. Who is gathering application functionality

information?

<--- Score

69. Are resources adequate for the scope?

<--- Score

70. What scope do you want your strategy to cover?

<--- Score

71. How would you define the culture at your organization, how susceptible is it to application functionality changes?

<--- Score

72. How do you keep key subject matter experts in the loop?

<--- Score

73. Have all basic functions of application functionality been defined?

<--- Score

74. Is there a critical path to deliver application functionality results?

<--- Score

75. How do you hand over application functionality context?

<--- Score

76. What is out of scope?

<--- Score

77. How do you gather requirements?

<--- Score

78. Do the problem and goal statements meet the SMART criteria (specific, measurable, attainable, relevant, and time-bound)?
<--- Score

79. How can the value of application functionality be defined?
<--- Score

80. Have the customer needs been translated into specific, measurable requirements? How?
<--- Score

81. Has a project plan, Gantt chart, or similar been developed/completed?
<--- Score

82. Has everyone on the team, including the team leaders, been properly trained?
<--- Score

83. How do you catch application functionality definition inconsistencies?
<--- Score

84. Who is gathering information?
<--- Score

85. How are consistent application functionality definitions important?
<--- Score

86. What intelligence can you gather?
<--- Score

87. Does the scope remain the same?
<--- Score

88. What application functionality services do you require?
<--- Score

89. Do you have organizational privacy requirements?
<--- Score

90. Has your scope been defined?
<--- Score

91. Has anyone else (internal or external to the group) attempted to solve this problem or a similar one before? If so, what knowledge can be leveraged from these previous efforts?
<--- Score

92. What is out-of-scope initially?
<--- Score

93. How did the application functionality manager receive input to the development of a application functionality improvement plan and the estimated completion dates/times of each activity?
<--- Score

94. Has a high-level 'as is' process map been completed, verified and validated?
<--- Score

95. Are audit criteria, scope, frequency and methods defined?
<--- Score

96. What is the context?
<--- Score

97. Will a application functionality production readiness review be required?
<--- Score

98. Is it clearly defined in and to your organization what you do?
<--- Score

99. Have all of the relationships been defined properly?
<--- Score

100. Is special application functionality user knowledge required?
<--- Score

101. How have you defined all application functionality requirements first?
<--- Score

102. How will the application functionality team and the group measure complete success of application functionality?
<--- Score

103. In what way can you redefine the criteria of choice clients have in your category in your favor?
<--- Score

104. Are required metrics defined, what are they?
<--- Score

105. Are approval levels defined for contracts and supplements to contracts?
<--- Score

106. What are the dynamics of the communication plan?
<--- Score

107. How do you manage changes in application functionality requirements?
<--- Score

108. What baselines are required to be defined and managed?
<--- Score

109. What are the compelling stakeholder reasons for embarking on application functionality?
<--- Score

110. What gets examined?
<--- Score

111. What information should you gather?
<--- Score

112. Has the improvement team collected the 'voice of the customer' (obtained feedback – qualitative and quantitative)?
<--- Score

113. How do you gather application functionality requirements?
<--- Score

114. Is the current 'as is' process being followed? If not,

what are the discrepancies?
<--- Score

115. Is the application functionality scope complete and appropriately sized?
<--- Score

116. Who defines (or who defined) the rules and roles?
<--- Score

117. If substitutes have been appointed, have they been briefed on the application functionality goals and received regular communications as to the progress to date?
<--- Score

118. What scope to assess?
<--- Score

119. When is the estimated completion date?
<--- Score

120. How will variation in the actual durations of each activity be dealt with to ensure that the expected application functionality results are met?
<--- Score

121. Is there a completed, verified, and validated high-level 'as is' (not 'should be' or 'could be') stakeholder process map?
<--- Score

122. What is the scope of the application functionality effort?
<--- Score

123. Are all requirements met?
<--- Score

124. Who are the application functionality improvement team members, including Management Leads and Coaches?
<--- Score

125. Is there a completed SIPOC representation, describing the Suppliers, Inputs, Process, Outputs, and Customers?
<--- Score

126. Is there a clear application functionality case definition?
<--- Score

127. What is a worst-case scenario for losses?
<--- Score

128. What are the boundaries of the scope? What is in bounds and what is not? What is the start point? What is the stop point?
<--- Score

129. How do you gather the stories?
<--- Score

130. What system do you use for gathering application functionality information?
<--- Score

131. Scope of sensitive information?
<--- Score

132. What is the definition of success?

<--- Score

133. How often are the team meetings?
<--- Score

134. Has the application functionality work been fairly and/or equitably divided and delegated among team members who are qualified and capable to perform the work? Has everyone contributed?
<--- Score

Add up total points for this section:
_____ = Total points for this section

Divided by: _____ (number of statements answered) = _____
Average score for this section

Transfer your score to the application functionality Index at the beginning of the Self-Assessment.

CRITERION #3: MEASURE:

INTENT: Gather the correct data.
Measure the current performance and
evolution of the situation.

In my belief, the answer to this
question is clearly defined:

5 Strongly Agree

4 Agree

3 Neutral

2 Disagree

1 Strongly Disagree

1. Has a cost center been established?
<--- Score

2. Are actual costs in line with budgeted costs?
<--- Score

3. How do you measure efficient delivery of
application functionality services?
<--- Score

4. How do you focus on what is right -not who is right?
<--- Score

5. Do you have any cost application functionality limitation requirements?
<--- Score

6. Does the application functionality task fit the client's priorities?
<--- Score

7. How much does it cost?
<--- Score

8. What are the costs?
<--- Score

9. What are the operational costs after application functionality deployment?
<--- Score

10. Who is involved in verifying compliance?
<--- Score

11. How frequently do you verify your application functionality strategy?
<--- Score

12. How to cause the change?
<--- Score

13. What is the total fixed cost?
<--- Score

14. What are the strategic priorities for this year?
<--- Score

15. Are you taking your company in the direction of better and revenue or cheaper and cost?
<--- Score

16. What are the current costs of the application functionality process?
<--- Score

17. What is your decision requirements diagram?
<--- Score

18. What are predictive application functionality analytics?
<--- Score

19. What is measured? Why?
<--- Score

20. When a disaster occurs, who gets priority?
<--- Score

21. How can you measure application functionality in a systematic way?
<--- Score

22. Are there measurements based on task performance?
<--- Score

23. How will measures be used to manage and adapt?
<--- Score

24. Among the application functionality product and

service cost to be estimated, which is considered hardest to estimate?
<--- Score

25. Was a business case (cost/benefit) developed?
<--- Score

26. What are allowable costs?
<--- Score

27. Are the application functionality benefits worth its costs?
<--- Score

28. Do you verify that corrective actions were taken?
<--- Score

29. How do you measure variability?
<--- Score

30. How are measurements made?
<--- Score

31. What is an unallowable cost?
<--- Score

32. What would be a real cause for concern?
<--- Score

33. Does management have the right priorities among projects?
<--- Score

34. What drives O&M cost?
<--- Score

35. What disadvantage does this cause for the user?
<--- Score

36. How can you manage cost down?
<--- Score

37. When are costs are incurred?
<--- Score

38. Are application functionality vulnerabilities categorized and prioritized?
<--- Score

39. What harm might be caused?
<--- Score

40. How will you measure success?
<--- Score

41. Do you have a flow diagram of what happens?
<--- Score

42. What causes innovation to fail or succeed in your organization?
<--- Score

43. Who pays the cost?
<--- Score

44. What would it cost to replace your technology?
<--- Score

45. Which measures and indicators matter?
<--- Score

46. What does verifying compliance entail?
<--- Score

47. What happens if cost savings do not materialize?
<--- Score

48. Where can you go to verify the info?
<--- Score

49. What are the costs of reform?
<--- Score

50. What potential environmental factors impact the application functionality effort?
<--- Score

51. Are you able to realize any cost savings?
<--- Score

52. What is the root cause(s) of the problem?
<--- Score

53. How do you verify and validate the application functionality data?
<--- Score

54. Why a application functionality focus?
<--- Score

55. How do you quantify and qualify impacts?
<--- Score

56. What are the uncertainties surrounding estimates of impact?
<--- Score

57. The approach of traditional application functionality works for detail complexity but is focused on a systematic approach rather than an understanding of the nature of systems themselves, what approach will permit your organization to deal with the kind of unpredictable emergent behaviors that dynamic complexity can introduce?
<--- Score

58. What could cause delays in the schedule?
<--- Score

59. How will you measure your application functionality effectiveness?
<--- Score

60. Do you have an issue in getting priority?
<--- Score

61. How do you measure success?
<--- Score

62. What are your primary costs, revenues, assets?
<--- Score

63. What are your customers expectations and measures?
<--- Score

64. How do you aggregate measures across priorities?
<--- Score

65. How are you verifying it?
<--- Score

66. What are your key application functionality organizational performance measures, including key short and longer-term financial measures?
<--- Score

67. Do you aggressively reward and promote the people who have the biggest impact on creating excellent application functionality services/products?
<--- Score

68. Which costs should be taken into account?
<--- Score

69. Do you effectively measure and reward individual and team performance?
<--- Score

70. Are indirect costs charged to the application functionality program?
<--- Score

71. Why do you expend time and effort to implement measurement, for whom?
<--- Score

72. How will your organization measure success?
<--- Score

73. What is the cost of rework?
<--- Score

74. Do the benefits outweigh the costs?
<--- Score

75. How will costs be allocated?
<--- Score

76. Are you aware of what could cause a problem?
<--- Score

77. How is progress measured?
<--- Score

78. What can be used to verify compliance?
<--- Score

79. How do you control the overall costs of your work processes?
<--- Score

80. How frequently do you track application functionality measures?
<--- Score

81. How do you verify the application functionality requirements quality?
<--- Score

82. Is a follow-up focused external application functionality review required?
<--- Score

83. Are there competing application functionality priorities?
<--- Score

84. Was a life-cycle cost analysis performed?
<--- Score

85. What methods are feasible and acceptable to estimate the impact of reforms?
<--- Score

86. What do you measure and why?
<--- Score

87. How can you reduce costs?
<--- Score

88. How will success or failure be measured?
<--- Score

89. What is the application functionality business impact?
<--- Score

90. What are the estimated costs of proposed changes?
<--- Score

91. How do your measurements capture actionable application functionality information for use in exceeding your customers expectations and securing your customers engagement?
<--- Score

92. What are the types and number of measures to use?
<--- Score

93. Are missed application functionality opportunities costing your organization money?
<--- Score

94. How can you measure the performance?
<--- Score

95. Did you tackle the cause or the symptom?

<--- Score

96. Are the measurements objective?
<--- Score

97. When should you bother with diagrams?
<--- Score

98. What are the costs of delaying application functionality action?
<--- Score

99. How is performance measured?
<--- Score

100. Have you made assumptions about the shape of the future, particularly its impact on your customers and competitors?
<--- Score

101. What is your application functionality quality cost segregation study?
<--- Score

102. What tests verify requirements?
<--- Score

103. How do you verify if application functionality is built right?
<--- Score

104. What could cause you to change course?
<--- Score

105. What does a Test Case verify?
<--- Score

106. What does losing customers cost your organization?

<--- Score

107. Where is the cost?

<--- Score

108. What are the application functionality investment costs?

<--- Score

109. What are you verifying?

<--- Score

110. Why do the measurements/indicators matter?

<--- Score

111. How will the application functionality data be analyzed?

<--- Score

112. Are there any easy-to-implement alternatives to application functionality? Sometimes other solutions are available that do not require the cost implications of a full-blown project?

<--- Score

113. Are supply costs steady or fluctuating?

<--- Score

114. Who should receive measurement reports?

<--- Score

115. What measurements are being captured?

<--- Score

116. How do you prevent mis-estimating cost?
<--- Score

117. Is the cost worth the application functionality effort ?
<--- Score

118. What are the application functionality key cost drivers?
<--- Score

119. What measurements are possible, practicable and meaningful?
<--- Score

120. How sensitive must the application functionality strategy be to cost?
<--- Score

121. How do you verify application functionality completeness and accuracy?
<--- Score

122. At what cost?
<--- Score

123. How can you reduce the costs of obtaining inputs?
<--- Score

124. How is the value delivered by application functionality being measured?
<--- Score

125. What are your operating costs?

<--- Score

126. What relevant entities could be measured?
<--- Score

127. Where is it measured?
<--- Score

128. How do you verify your resources?
<--- Score

129. What do people want to verify?
<--- Score

130. How do you verify the authenticity of the data and information used?
<--- Score

131. What causes extra work or rework?
<--- Score

132. Is there an opportunity to verify requirements?
<--- Score

133. What does your operating model cost?
<--- Score

134. How do you measure lifecycle phases?
<--- Score

135. How do you verify performance?
<--- Score

136. How do you verify and develop ideas and innovations?
<--- Score

137. Does a application functionality quantification method exist?

<--- Score

138. What are hidden application functionality quality costs?

<--- Score

139. How do you stay flexible and focused to recognize larger application functionality results?

<--- Score

140. What are the costs and benefits?

<--- Score

141. How are costs allocated?

<--- Score

Add up total points for this section:
_ _ _ _ _ = Total points for this section

Divided by: _ _ _ _ _ _ (number of statements answered) = _ _ _ _ _ _
Average score for this section

Transfer your score to the application functionality Index at the beginning of the Self-Assessment.

CRITERION #4: ANALYZE:

INTENT: Analyze causes, assumptions and hypotheses.

In my belief, the answer to this question is clearly defined:

5 Strongly Agree

4 Agree

3 Neutral

2 Disagree

1 Strongly Disagree

1. How will the change process be managed?
<--- Score

2. Is the required application functionality data gathered?
<--- Score

3. What data is gathered?
<--- Score

4. What other jobs or tasks affect the performance of the steps in the application functionality process?
<--- Score

5. What is the complexity of the output produced?
<--- Score

6. What is the oversight process?
<--- Score

7. How do your work systems and key work processes relate to and capitalize on your core competencies?
<--- Score

8. How can risk management be tied procedurally to process elements?
<--- Score

9. What data do you need to collect?
<--- Score

10. Do staff qualifications match your project?
<--- Score

11. How much data can be collected in the given timeframe?
<--- Score

12. What training and qualifications will you need?
<--- Score

13. What are your current levels and trends in key measures or indicators of application functionality product and process performance that are important to and directly serve your customers? How do these results compare with the performance of your

competitors and other organizations with similar offerings?
<--- Score

14. How will the application functionality data be captured?
<--- Score

15. Have you defined which data is gathered how?
<--- Score

16. Is pre-qualification of suppliers carried out?
<--- Score

17. What is the cost of poor quality as supported by the team's analysis?
<--- Score

18. What types of data do your application functionality indicators require?
<--- Score

19. Where can you get qualified talent today?
<--- Score

20. What will drive application functionality change?
<--- Score

21. Which application functionality data should be retained?
<--- Score

22. What are the personnel training and qualifications required?
<--- Score

23. What internal processes need improvement?
<--- Score

24. Are you missing application functionality opportunities?
<--- Score

25. What successful thing are you doing today that may be blinding you to new growth opportunities?
<--- Score

26. Do your leaders quickly bounce back from setbacks?
<--- Score

27. How do you use application functionality data and information to support organizational decision making and innovation?
<--- Score

28. What are the application functionality business drivers?
<--- Score

29. Who will gather what data?
<--- Score

30. Do you, as a leader, bounce back quickly from setbacks?
<--- Score

31. What other organizational variables, such as reward systems or communication systems, affect the performance of this application functionality process?
<--- Score

32. Where is the data coming from to measure compliance?
<--- Score

33. Have any additional benefits been identified that will result from closing all or most of the gaps?
<--- Score

34. How does the organization define, manage, and improve its application functionality processes?
<--- Score

35. Has an output goal been set?
<--- Score

36. What conclusions were drawn from the team's data collection and analysis? How did the team reach these conclusions?
<--- Score

37. Was a cause-and-effect diagram used to explore the different types of causes (or sources of variation)?
<--- Score

38. How many input/output points does it require?
<--- Score

39. Who is involved in the management review process?
<--- Score

40. What are evaluation criteria for the output?
<--- Score

41. Is the gap/opportunity displayed and

communicated in financial terms?

<--- Score

42. Has data output been validated?

<--- Score

43. Who qualifies to gain access to data?

<--- Score

44. Were there any improvement opportunities identified from the process analysis?

<--- Score

45. What are your key performance measures or indicators and in-process measures for the control and improvement of your application functionality processes?

<--- Score

46. What are the revised rough estimates of the financial savings/opportunity for application functionality improvements?

<--- Score

47. Is the final output clearly identified?

<--- Score

48. Is there a strict change management process?

<--- Score

49. Is the suppliers process defined and controlled?

<--- Score

50. What tools were used to generate the list of possible causes?

<--- Score

51. Should you invest in industry-recognized qualifications?
<--- Score

52. What were the crucial 'moments of truth' on the process map?
<--- Score

53. How do you implement and manage your work processes to ensure that they meet design requirements?
<--- Score

54. Where is application functionality data gathered?
<--- Score

55. What controls do you have in place to protect data?
<--- Score

56. How difficult is it to qualify what application functionality ROI is?
<--- Score

57. How are outputs preserved and protected?
<--- Score

58. What qualifications do application functionality leaders need?
<--- Score

59. Do you have the authority to produce the output?
<--- Score

60. How has the application functionality data

been gathered?
<--- Score

61. What kind of crime could a potential new hire
have committed that would not only not disqualify
him/her from being hired by your organization,
but would actually indicate that he/she might be a
particularly good fit?
<--- Score

62. What did the team gain from developing a sub-
process map?
<--- Score

63. What does the data say about the performance of
the stakeholder process?
<--- Score

64. Have the problem and goal statements been
updated to reflect the additional knowledge gained
from the analyze phase?
<--- Score

65. Did any additional data need to be collected?
<--- Score

66. Are all staff in core application functionality
subjects Highly Qualified?
<--- Score

67. Were Pareto charts (or similar) used to portray the
'heavy hitters' (or key sources of variation)?
<--- Score

68. How is application functionality data gathered?
<--- Score

69. How often will data be collected for measures?
<--- Score

70. Is the application functionality process severely broken such that a re-design is necessary?
<--- Score

71. What resources go in to get the desired output?
<--- Score

72. What qualifications and skills do you need?
<--- Score

73. What process improvements will be needed?
<--- Score

74. How do mission and objectives affect the application functionality processes of your organization?
<--- Score

75. Are gaps between current performance and the goal performance identified?
<--- Score

76. Are application functionality changes recognized early enough to be approved through the regular process?
<--- Score

77. When should a process be art not science?
<--- Score

78. What is the application functionality Driver?
<--- Score

79. What are your outputs?
<--- Score

80. What are your best practices for minimizing application functionality project risk, while demonstrating incremental value and quick wins throughout the application functionality project lifecycle?
<--- Score

81. What application functionality metrics are outputs of the process?
<--- Score

82. What are your application functionality processes?
<--- Score

83. What are your current levels and trends in key application functionality measures or indicators of product and process performance that are important to and directly serve your customers?
<--- Score

84. Do several people in different organizational units assist with the application functionality process?
<--- Score

85. Who gets your output?
<--- Score

86. What do you need to qualify?
<--- Score

87. Is the performance gap determined?
<--- Score

88. What qualifies as competition?
<--- Score

89. What information qualified as important?
<--- Score

90. Think about the functions involved in your application functionality project, what processes flow from these functions?
<--- Score

91. Do your contracts/agreements contain data security obligations?
<--- Score

92. Is there any way to speed up the process?
<--- Score

93. How is the application functionality Value Stream Mapping managed?
<--- Score

94. Do you understand your management processes today?
<--- Score

95. What qualifications are necessary?
<--- Score

96. What is your organizations process which leads to recognition of value generation?
<--- Score

97. Who will facilitate the team and process?
<--- Score

98. Who owns what data?
<--- Score

99. What is your organizations system for selecting qualified vendors?
<--- Score

100. How do you promote understanding that opportunity for improvement is not criticism of the status quo, or the people who created the status quo?
<--- Score

101. What application functionality data should be collected?
<--- Score

102. What is the Value Stream Mapping?
<--- Score

103. Who is involved with workflow mapping?
<--- Score

104. Were any designed experiments used to generate additional insight into the data analysis?
<--- Score

105. Think about some of the processes you undertake within your organization, which do you own?
<--- Score

106. How do you identify specific application functionality investment opportunities and emerging trends?
<--- Score

107. How will corresponding data be collected?
<--- Score

108. Is data and process analysis, root cause analysis and quantifying the gap/opportunity in place?
<--- Score

109. What process should you select for improvement?
<--- Score

110. Did any value-added analysis or 'lean thinking' take place to identify some of the gaps shown on the 'as is' process map?
<--- Score

111. How do you define collaboration and team output?
<--- Score

112. What is the output?
<--- Score

113. Are your outputs consistent?
<--- Score

114. Can you add value to the current application functionality decision-making process (largely qualitative) by incorporating uncertainty modeling (more quantitative)?
<--- Score

115. Record-keeping requirements flow from the records needed as inputs, outputs, controls and for transformation of a application functionality process,

are the records needed as inputs to the application functionality process available?
<--- Score

116. What, related to, application functionality processes does your organization outsource?
<--- Score

117. Identify an operational issue in your organization, for example, could a particular task be done more quickly or more efficiently by application functionality?
<--- Score

118. What are the disruptive application functionality technologies that enable your organization to radically change your business processes?
<--- Score

119. What tools were used to narrow the list of possible causes?
<--- Score

120. Are all team members qualified for all tasks?
<--- Score

121. What were the financial benefits resulting from any 'ground fruit or low-hanging fruit' (quick fixes)?
<--- Score

122. How do you measure the operational performance of your key work systems and processes, including productivity, cycle time, and other appropriate measures of process effectiveness, efficiency, and innovation?
<--- Score

123. How is data used for program management and improvement?
<--- Score

124. What methods do you use to gather application functionality data?
<--- Score

125. How is the data gathered?
<--- Score

126. What quality tools were used to get through the analyze phase?
<--- Score

127. What are the best opportunities for value improvement?
<--- Score

128. How do you ensure that the application functionality opportunity is realistic?
<--- Score

129. An organizationally feasible system request is one that considers the mission, goals and objectives of the organization, key questions are: is the application functionality solution request practical and will it solve a problem or take advantage of an opportunity to achieve company goals?
<--- Score

130. How will the data be checked for quality?
<--- Score

131. What application functionality data do you

gather or use now?
<--- Score

132. How was the detailed process map generated, verified, and validated?
<--- Score

133. Was a detailed process map created to amplify critical steps of the 'as is' stakeholder process?
<--- Score

Add up total points for this section:
_____ = Total points for this section

Divided by: _____ (number of statements answered) = _____
Average score for this section

Transfer your score to the application functionality Index at the beginning of the Self-Assessment.

CRITERION #5: IMPROVE:

INTENT: Develop a practical solution.
Innovate, establish and test the
solution and to measure the results.

In my belief, the answer to this
question is clearly defined:

5 Strongly Agree

4 Agree

3 Neutral

2 Disagree

1 Strongly Disagree

1. Who will be responsible for documenting the application functionality requirements in detail?
<--- Score

2. Do vendor agreements bring new compliance risk ?
<--- Score

3. What application functionality improvements

can be made?
<--- Score

4. How is knowledge sharing about risk management improved?
<--- Score

5. How do you improve your likelihood of success ?
<--- Score

6. application functionality risk decisions: whose call Is It?
<--- Score

7. Is application functionality documentation maintained?
<--- Score

8. What resources are required for the improvement efforts?
<--- Score

9. What went well, what should change, what can improve?
<--- Score

10. How will you measure the results?
<--- Score

11. Which of the recognised risks out of all risks can be most likely transferred?
<--- Score

12. How do you measure risk?
<--- Score

13. What strategies for application functionality improvement are successful?
<--- Score

14. Have you achieved application functionality improvements?
<--- Score

15. When you map the key players in your own work and the types/domains of relationships with them, which relationships do you find easy and which challenging, and why?
<--- Score

16. Who are the application functionality decision-makers?
<--- Score

17. Is the measure of success for application functionality understandable to a variety of people?
<--- Score

18. How significant is the improvement in the eyes of the end user?
<--- Score

19. Do you cover the five essential competencies: Communication, Collaboration,Innovation, Adaptability, and Leadership that improve an organizations ability to leverage the new application functionality in a volatile global economy?
<--- Score

20. What improvements have been achieved?
<--- Score

21. Can you integrate quality management and risk management?
<--- Score

22. How will you know when its improved?
<--- Score

23. What actually has to improve and by how much?
<--- Score

24. How will you recognize and celebrate results?
<--- Score

25. What are the affordable application functionality risks?
<--- Score

26. What tools were used to tap into the creativity and encourage 'outside the box' thinking?
<--- Score

27. For estimation problems, how do you develop an estimation statement?
<--- Score

28. How do the application functionality results compare with the performance of your competitors and other organizations with similar offerings?
<--- Score

29. How can the phases of application functionality development be identified?
<--- Score

30. Risk events: what are the things that could go

wrong?
<--- Score

31. Who are the application functionality decision makers?
<--- Score

32. How risky is your organization?
<--- Score

33. Who controls key decisions that will be made?
<--- Score

34. What is the application functionality's sustainability risk?
<--- Score

35. Would you develop a application functionality Communication Strategy?
<--- Score

36. Where do the application functionality decisions reside?
<--- Score

37. What tools were most useful during the improve phase?
<--- Score

38. How scalable is your application functionality solution?
<--- Score

39. Was a application functionality charter developed?
<--- Score

40. What communications are necessary to support the implementation of the solution?
<--- Score

41. What needs improvement? Why?
<--- Score

42. What to do with the results or outcomes of measurements?
<--- Score

43. Risk Identification: What are the possible risk events your organization faces in relation to application functionality?
<--- Score

44. To what extent does management recognize application functionality as a tool to increase the results?
<--- Score

45. Are the risks fully understood, reasonable and manageable?
<--- Score

46. What should a proof of concept or pilot accomplish?
<--- Score

47. What risks do you need to manage?
<--- Score

48. How do you mitigate application functionality risk?
<--- Score

49. Who makes the application functionality decisions in your organization?

<--- Score

50. Is supporting application functionality documentation required?

<--- Score

51. What area needs the greatest improvement?

<--- Score

52. What practices helps your organization to develop its capacity to recognize patterns?

<--- Score

53. What is the team's contingency plan for potential problems occurring in implementation?

<--- Score

54. Risk factors: what are the characteristics of application functionality that make it risky?

<--- Score

55. What does the 'should be' process map/design look like?

<--- Score

56. Are events managed to resolution?

<--- Score

57. Is the application functionality risk managed?

<--- Score

58. How do you keep improving application functionality?

<--- Score

59. Who manages application functionality risk?
<--- Score

60. Have you identified breakpoints and/or risk tolerances that will trigger broad consideration of a potential need for intervention or modification of strategy?
<--- Score

61. What attendant changes will need to be made to ensure that the solution is successful?
<--- Score

62. Are risk management tasks balanced centrally and locally?
<--- Score

63. How do you measure improved application functionality service perception, and satisfaction?
<--- Score

64. In the past few months, what is the smallest change you have made that has had the biggest positive result? What was it about that small change that produced the large return?
<--- Score

65. Who manages supplier risk management in your organization?
<--- Score

66. Do you need to do a usability evaluation?
<--- Score

67. What were the underlying assumptions on the

cost-benefit analysis?
<--- Score

68. What is the risk?
<--- Score

69. For decision problems, how do you develop a decision statement?
<--- Score

70. How are application functionality risks managed?
<--- Score

71. Are decisions made in a timely manner?
<--- Score

72. Are the key business and technology risks being managed?
<--- Score

73. Is the scope clearly documented?
<--- Score

74. Why improve in the first place?
<--- Score

75. Do you combine technical expertise with business knowledge and application functionality Key topics include lifecycles, development approaches, requirements and how to make a business case?
<--- Score

76. How can you better manage risk?
<--- Score

77. Can the solution be designed and

implemented within an acceptable time period?
<--- Score

78. Does the goal represent a desired result that can
be measured?
<--- Score

79. Where do you need application functionality
improvement?
<--- Score

80. What do you want to improve?
<--- Score

81. Who should make the application functionality
decisions?
<--- Score

82. Are risk triggers captured?
<--- Score

83. How does your organization evaluate strategic
application functionality success?
<--- Score

**84. Is there a high likelihood that any
recommendations will achieve their intended
results?**
<--- Score

85. Is any application functionality documentation
required?
<--- Score

86. What is the magnitude of the improvements?
<--- Score

87. Are procedures documented for managing application functionality risks?
<--- Score

88. Who are the key stakeholders for the application functionality evaluation?
<--- Score

89. How can skill-level changes improve application functionality?
<--- Score

90. How can you improve application functionality?
<--- Score

91. Who do you report application functionality results to?
<--- Score

92. What lessons, if any, from a pilot were incorporated into the design of the full-scale solution?
<--- Score

93. What is application functionality's impact on utilizing the best solution(s)?
<--- Score

94. What is the implementation plan?
<--- Score

95. What alternative responses are available to manage risk?
<--- Score

96. How will you know that you have improved?
<--- Score

97. What criteria will you use to assess your application functionality risks?
<--- Score

98. What were the criteria for evaluating a application functionality pilot?
<--- Score

99. How do you manage and improve your application functionality work systems to deliver customer value and achieve organizational success and sustainability?
<--- Score

100. Is risk periodically assessed?
<--- Score

101. How do you measure progress and evaluate training effectiveness?
<--- Score

102. How do you manage application functionality risk?
<--- Score

103. What current systems have to be understood and/or changed?
<--- Score

104. What tools were used to evaluate the potential solutions?
<--- Score

105. How does the team improve its work?
<--- Score

106. Which application functionality solution is appropriate?
<--- Score

107. Who will be responsible for making the decisions to include or exclude requested changes once application functionality is underway?
<--- Score

108. How will you know that a change is an improvement?
<--- Score

109. If you could go back in time five years, what decision would you make differently? What is your best guess as to what decision you're making today you might regret five years from now?
<--- Score

110. Do those selected for the application functionality team have a good general understanding of what application functionality is all about?
<--- Score

111. Does a good decision guarantee a good outcome?
<--- Score

112. How can you improve performance?
<--- Score

113. How do you improve application functionality

service perception, and satisfaction?
<--- Score

114. How do you improve productivity?
<--- Score

115. Who controls the risk?
<--- Score

116. Explorations of the frontiers of application functionality will help you build influence, improve application functionality, optimize decision making, and sustain change, what is your approach?
<--- Score

117. Were any criteria developed to assist the team in testing and evaluating potential solutions?
<--- Score

118. What error proofing will be done to address some of the discrepancies observed in the 'as is' process?
<--- Score

119. How do you go about comparing application functionality approaches/solutions?
<--- Score

120. How do you link measurement and risk?
<--- Score

121. Is the application functionality documentation thorough?
<--- Score

122. What can you do to improve?
<--- Score

123. What are the concrete application functionality results?
<--- Score

124. Will the controls trigger any other risks?
<--- Score

125. Who are the people involved in developing and implementing application functionality?
<--- Score

126. How do you deal with application functionality risk?
<--- Score

127. Can you identify any significant risks or exposures to application functionality third-parties (vendors, service providers, alliance partners etc) that concern you?
<--- Score

128. Who will be using the results of the measurement activities?
<--- Score

129. Is the solution technically practical?
<--- Score

130. How do you define the solutions' scope?
<--- Score

131. At what point will vulnerability assessments be performed once application functionality is put into production (e.g., ongoing Risk Management after implementation)?

<--- Score

132. Are you assessing application functionality and risk?
<--- Score

133. How is continuous improvement applied to risk management?
<--- Score

134. What are the implications of the one critical application functionality decision 10 minutes, 10 months, and 10 years from now?
<--- Score

Add up total points for this section:
_ _ _ _ _ = Total points for this section

Divided by: _ _ _ _ _ _ (number of statements answered) = _ _ _ _ _ _
Average score for this section

Transfer your score to the application functionality Index at the beginning of the Self-Assessment.

CRITERION #6: CONTROL:

INTENT: Implement the practical solution. Maintain the performance and correct possible complications.

In my belief, the answer to this question is clearly defined:

5 Strongly Agree

4 Agree

3 Neutral

2 Disagree

1 Strongly Disagree

1. Is a response plan in place for when the input, process, or output measures indicate an 'out-of-control' condition?
<--- Score

2. Are controls in place and consistently applied?
<--- Score

3. What is the best design framework for application

functionality organization now that, in a post industrial-age if the top-down, command and control model is no longer relevant?

<--- Score

4. Does the response plan contain a definite closed loop continual improvement scheme (e.g., plan-do-check-act)?

<--- Score

5. Will the team be available to assist members in planning investigations?

<--- Score

6. What are the performance and scale of the application functionality tools?

<--- Score

7. Implementation Planning: is a pilot needed to test the changes before a full roll out occurs?

<--- Score

8. Who will be in control?

<--- Score

9. Is there a control plan in place for sustaining improvements (short and long-term)?

<--- Score

10. How do senior leaders actions reflect a commitment to the organizations application functionality values?

<--- Score

11. What is the recommended frequency of auditing?

<--- Score

12. How do you monitor usage and cost?
<--- Score

13. Will any special training be provided for results interpretation?
<--- Score

14. What application functionality standards are applicable?
<--- Score

15. In the case of a application functionality project, the criteria for the audit derive from implementation objectives, an audit of a application functionality project involves assessing whether the recommendations outlined for implementation have been met, can you track that any application functionality project is implemented as planned, and is it working?
<--- Score

16. Who sets the application functionality standards?
<--- Score

17. Does the application functionality performance meet the customer's requirements?
<--- Score

18. How will the process owner and team be able to hold the gains?
<--- Score

19. You may have created your quality measures at a time when you lacked resources, technology wasn't up to the required standard, or low service levels

were the industry norm. Have those circumstances changed?
<--- Score

20. What do you stand for--and what are you against?
<--- Score

21. Are pertinent alerts monitored, analyzed and distributed to appropriate personnel?
<--- Score

22. Are the planned controls working?
<--- Score

23. Has the improved process and its steps been standardized?
<--- Score

24. How do you plan on providing proper recognition and disclosure of supporting companies?
<--- Score

25. Is there an action plan in case of emergencies?
<--- Score

26. Have new or revised work instructions resulted?
<--- Score

27. What is your theory of human motivation, and how does your compensation plan fit with that view?
<--- Score

28. Is there a standardized process?
<--- Score

29. What do you measure to verify effectiveness

gains?
<--- Score

30. How will input, process, and output variables be checked to detect for sub-optimal conditions?
<--- Score

31. What adjustments to the strategies are needed?
<--- Score

32. Is a response plan established and deployed?
<--- Score

33. Is there documentation that will support the successful operation of the improvement?
<--- Score

34. Can you adapt and adjust to changing application functionality situations?
<--- Score

35. What other systems, operations, processes, and infrastructures (hiring practices, staffing, training, incentives/rewards, metrics/dashboards/scorecards, etc.) need updates, additions, changes, or deletions in order to facilitate knowledge transfer and improvements?
<--- Score

36. What quality tools were useful in the control phase?
<--- Score

37. Are operating procedures consistent?
<--- Score

38. How can you best use all of your knowledge repositories to enhance learning and sharing?
<--- Score

39. Can support from partners be adjusted?
<--- Score

40. What is the standard for acceptable application functionality performance?
<--- Score

41. Where do ideas that reach policy makers and planners as proposals for application functionality strengthening and reform actually originate?
<--- Score

42. What other areas of the group might benefit from the application functionality team's improvements, knowledge, and learning?
<--- Score

43. How do your controls stack up?
<--- Score

44. How is application functionality project cost planned, managed, monitored?
<--- Score

45. Is reporting being used or needed?
<--- Score

46. Is there a application functionality Communication plan covering who needs to get what information when?
<--- Score

47. Act/Adjust: What Do you Need to Do Differently?
<--- Score

48. Will existing staff require re-training, for example, to learn new business processes?
<--- Score

49. How likely is the current application functionality plan to come in on schedule or on budget?
<--- Score

50. How will new or emerging customer needs/ requirements be checked/communicated to orient the process toward meeting the new specifications and continually reducing variation?
<--- Score

51. How will report readings be checked to effectively monitor performance?
<--- Score

52. Is new knowledge gained imbedded in the response plan?
<--- Score

53. How do you select, collect, align, and integrate application functionality data and information for tracking daily operations and overall organizational performance, including progress relative to strategic objectives and action plans?
<--- Score

54. Are you measuring, monitoring and predicting application functionality activities to optimize operations and profitability, and enhancing

outcomes?
<--- Score

55. How do controls support value?
<--- Score

56. Who is going to spread your message?
<--- Score

57. Are the planned controls in place?
<--- Score

58. Are new process steps, standards, and documentation ingrained into normal operations?
<--- Score

59. How will the process owner verify improvement in present and future sigma levels, process capabilities?
<--- Score

60. Who controls critical resources?
<--- Score

61. Are the application functionality standards challenging?
<--- Score

62. What is your plan to assess your security risks?
<--- Score

63. Do you monitor the effectiveness of your application functionality activities?
<--- Score

64. What are the critical parameters to watch?
<--- Score

65. Does job training on the documented procedures need to be part of the process team's education and training?
<--- Score

66. Does a troubleshooting guide exist or is it needed?
<--- Score

67. How will you measure your QA plan's effectiveness?
<--- Score

68. Are documented procedures clear and easy to follow for the operators?
<--- Score

69. Who is the application functionality process owner?
<--- Score

70. What key inputs and outputs are being measured on an ongoing basis?
<--- Score

71. What are customers monitoring?
<--- Score

72. Do the viable solutions scale to future needs?
<--- Score

73. Who has control over resources?
<--- Score

74. What are the known security controls?
<--- Score

75. Has the application functionality value of standards been quantified?
<--- Score

76. What are your results for key measures or indicators of the accomplishment of your application functionality strategy and action plans, including building and strengthening core competencies?
<--- Score

77. Do the application functionality decisions you make today help people and the planet tomorrow?
<--- Score

78. Is there a recommended audit plan for routine surveillance inspections of application functionality's gains?
<--- Score

79. Is there a transfer of ownership and knowledge to process owner and process team tasked with the responsibilities.
<--- Score

80. What should you measure to verify efficiency gains?
<--- Score

81. Are there documented procedures?
<--- Score

82. Is there a documented and implemented monitoring plan?
<--- Score

83. How is change control managed?
<--- Score

84. Against what alternative is success being measured?
<--- Score

85. What should the next improvement project be that is related to application functionality?
<--- Score

86. What can you control?
<--- Score

87. What is the control/monitoring plan?
<--- Score

88. What are you attempting to measure/monitor?
<--- Score

89. How widespread is its use?
<--- Score

90. Will your goals reflect your program budget?
<--- Score

91. What are the key elements of your application functionality performance improvement system, including your evaluation, organizational learning, and innovation processes?
<--- Score

92. How might the group capture best practices and lessons learned so as to leverage improvements?
<--- Score

93. How will application functionality decisions be made and monitored?

<--- Score

94. Does application functionality appropriately measure and monitor risk?

<--- Score

95. Is knowledge gained on process shared and institutionalized?

<--- Score

96. Are suggested corrective/restorative actions indicated on the response plan for known causes to problems that might surface?

<--- Score

97. How will the day-to-day responsibilities for monitoring and continual improvement be transferred from the improvement team to the process owner?

<--- Score

98. How do you encourage people to take control and responsibility?

<--- Score

99. How do you spread information?

<--- Score

Add up total points for this section:
_ _ _ _ _ = Total points for this section

Divided by: _ _ _ _ _ _ (number of statements answered) = _ _ _ _ _ _

Average score for this section

Transfer your score to the application
functionality Index at the beginning of
the Self-Assessment.

CRITERION #7: SUSTAIN:

INTENT: Retain the benefits.

In my belief, the answer to this question is clearly defined:

5 Strongly Agree

4 Agree

3 Neutral

2 Disagree

1 Strongly Disagree

1. What could happen if you do not do it?
<--- Score

2. How can you negotiate application functionality successfully with a stubborn boss, an irate client, or a deceitful coworker?
<--- Score

3. How do you provide a safe environment -physically and emotionally?
<--- Score

4. How do you create buy-in?
<--- Score

5. What may be the consequences for the performance of an organization if all stakeholders are not consulted regarding application functionality?
<--- Score

6. What relationships among application functionality trends do you perceive?
<--- Score

7. How do you transition from the baseline to the target?
<--- Score

8. What is your BATNA (best alternative to a negotiated agreement)?
<--- Score

9. What happens at your organization when people fail?
<--- Score

10. What was the last experiment you ran?
<--- Score

11. What did you miss in the interview for the worst hire you ever made?
<--- Score

12. What are the challenges?
<--- Score

13. What is the craziest thing you can do?
<--- Score

14. What must you excel at?
<--- Score

15. How will you motivate the stakeholders with the least vested interest?
<--- Score

16. Do you have the right capabilities and capacities?
<--- Score

17. In the past year, what have you done (or could you have done) to increase the accurate perception of your company/brand as ethical and honest?
<--- Score

18. If you weren't already in this business, would you enter it today? And if not, what are you going to do about it?
<--- Score

19. Who do you think the world wants your organization to be?
<--- Score

20. What happens if you do not have enough funding?
<--- Score

21. Do you have enough freaky customers in your portfolio pushing you to the limit day in and day out?

<--- Score

22. Ask yourself: how would you do this work if you only had one staff member to do it?
<--- Score

23. Why should people listen to you?
<--- Score

24. Whom among your colleagues do you trust, and for what?
<--- Score

25. Do you know what you are doing? And who do you call if you don't?
<--- Score

26. How long will it take to change?
<--- Score

27. Are all key stakeholders present at all Structured Walkthroughs?
<--- Score

28. What is the overall talent health of your organization as a whole at senior levels, and for each organization reporting to a member of the Senior Leadership Team?
<--- Score

29. How are you doing compared to your industry?
<--- Score

30. How do you make it meaningful in connecting application functionality with what users do day-to-day?

<--- Score

31. How will you insure seamless interoperability of application functionality moving forward?
<--- Score

32. Which individuals, teams or departments will be involved in application functionality?
<--- Score

33. Who is responsible for application functionality?
<--- Score

34. Is a application functionality team work effort in place?
<--- Score

35. If you had to rebuild your organization without any traditional competitive advantages (i.e., no killer technology, promising research, innovative product/ service delivery model, etcetera), how would your people have to approach their work and collaborate together in order to create the necessary conditions for success?
<--- Score

36. Do you see more potential in people than they do in themselves?
<--- Score

37. Are you / should you be revolutionary or evolutionary?
<--- Score

38. Who will be responsible for deciding whether

**application functionality goes ahead or not after
the initial investigations?**
<--- Score

39. What are the essentials of internal application
functionality management?
<--- Score

40. What does your signature ensure?
<--- Score

**41. If you got fired and a new hire took your place,
what would she do different?**
<--- Score

42. If no one would ever find out about your
accomplishments, how would you lead differently?
<--- Score

**43. If there were zero limitations, what would you
do differently?**
<--- Score

44. How do you keep records, of what?
<--- Score

45. How do you know if you are successful?
<--- Score

**46. How do you engage the workforce, in addition
to satisfying them?**
<--- Score

47. Think of your application functionality project,
what are the main functions?
<--- Score

48. What happens when a new employee joins the organization?
<--- Score

49. What application functionality skills are most important?
<--- Score

50. How will you ensure you get what you expected?
<--- Score

51. What is the estimated value of the project?
<--- Score

52. What are you trying to prove to yourself, and how might it be hijacking your life and business success?
<--- Score

53. How much contingency will be available in the budget?
<--- Score

54. Do you know who is a friend or a foe?
<--- Score

55. Who uses your product in ways you never expected?
<--- Score

56. Is there any existing application functionality governance structure?
<--- Score

57. What new services of functionality will be implemented next with application functionality ?

<--- Score

58. Are you maintaining a past–present–future perspective throughout the application functionality discussion?
<--- Score

59. Are the criteria for selecting recommendations stated?
<--- Score

60. What are the business goals application functionality is aiming to achieve?
<--- Score

61. What are the top 3 things at the forefront of your application functionality agendas for the next 3 years?
<--- Score

62. How do you lead with application functionality in mind?
<--- Score

63. Who, on the executive team or the board, has spoken to a customer recently?
<--- Score

64. Whose voice (department, ethnic group, women, older workers, etc) might you have missed hearing from in your company, and how might you amplify this voice to create positive momentum for your business?
<--- Score

65. How do you go about securing application

functionality?

<--- Score

66. What management system can you use to leverage the application functionality experience, ideas, and concerns of the people closest to the work to be done?

<--- Score

67. Are you making progress, and are you making progress as application functionality leaders?

<--- Score

68. How do you proactively clarify deliverables and application functionality quality expectations?

<--- Score

69. How do you ensure that implementations of application functionality products are done in a way that ensures safety?

<--- Score

70. Political -is anyone trying to undermine this project?

<--- Score

71. What are the short and long-term application functionality goals?

<--- Score

72. What information is critical to your organization that your executives are ignoring?

<--- Score

73. Why will customers want to buy your organizations products/services?

<--- Score

74. What is effective application functionality?
<--- Score

75. Who do we want your customers to become?
<--- Score

76. Will it be accepted by users?
<--- Score

77. What would you recommend your friend do if he/she were facing this dilemma?
<--- Score

78. How do you deal with application functionality changes?
<--- Score

79. Is your basic point _____ or _____?
<--- Score

80. What are you challenging?
<--- Score

81. Are there any activities that you can take off your to do list?
<--- Score

82. What is an unauthorized commitment?
<--- Score

83. How do senior leaders deploy your organizations vision and values through your leadership system, to the workforce, to key suppliers and partners, and to customers and

other stakeholders, as appropriate?
<--- Score

84. Who will provide the final approval of application functionality deliverables?
<--- Score

85. What is the recommended frequency of auditing?
<--- Score

86. What is a feasible sequencing of reform initiatives over time?
<--- Score

87. Is it economical; do you have the time and money?
<--- Score

88. How important is application functionality to the user organizations mission?
<--- Score

89. What are your most important goals for the strategic application functionality objectives?
<--- Score

90. How do customers see your organization?
<--- Score

91. Is your strategy driving your strategy? Or is the way in which you allocate resources driving your strategy?
<--- Score

92. What is your application functionality strategy?
<--- Score

93. What stupid rule would you most like to kill?
<--- Score

94. What will be the consequences to the stakeholder (financial, reputation etc) if application functionality does not go ahead or fails to deliver the objectives?
<--- Score

95. What have been your experiences in defining long range application functionality goals?
<--- Score

96. What potential megatrends could make your business model obsolete?
<--- Score

97. Can you do all this work?
<--- Score

98. Who have you, as a company, historically been when you've been at your best?
<--- Score

99. What is the purpose of application functionality in relation to the mission?
<--- Score

100. Can the schedule be done in the given time?
<--- Score

101. What role does communication play in the success or failure of a application functionality project?
<--- Score

102. Which models, tools and techniques are

necessary?
<--- Score

103. Who is on the team?
<--- Score

104. Is there any reason to believe the opposite of my current belief?
<--- Score

105. Did your employees make progress today?
<--- Score

106. How do you keep the momentum going?
<--- Score

107. What are the barriers to increased application functionality production?
<--- Score

108. What are your personal philosophies regarding application functionality and how do they influence your work?
<--- Score

109. Operational - will it work?
<--- Score

110. What is the funding source for this project?
<--- Score

111. Why not do application functionality?
<--- Score

112. What trophy do you want on your mantle?
<--- Score

113. Would you rather sell to knowledgeable and informed customers or to uninformed customers?
<--- Score

114. What is the source of the strategies for application functionality strengthening and reform?
<--- Score

115. Is application functionality realistic, or are you setting yourself up for failure?
<--- Score

116. Do you have an implicit bias for capital investments over people investments?
<--- Score

117. Who are the key stakeholders?
<--- Score

118. How can you become the company that would put you out of business?
<--- Score

119. If you do not follow, then how to lead?
<--- Score

120. How is implementation research currently incorporated into each of your goals?
<--- Score

121. How do you foster innovation?
<--- Score

122. Are the assumptions believable and achievable?
<--- Score

123. What are the key enablers to make this application functionality move?
<--- Score

124. What are the gaps in your knowledge and experience?
<--- Score

125. Do you have the right people on the bus?
<--- Score

126. What counts that you are not counting?
<--- Score

127. Do you think you know, or do you know you know ?
<--- Score

128. How do you accomplish your long range application functionality goals?
<--- Score

129. Marketing budgets are tighter, consumers are more skeptical, and social media has changed forever the way we talk about application functionality, how do you gain traction?
<--- Score

130. What should you stop doing?
<--- Score

131. What have you done to protect your business from competitive encroachment?
<--- Score

132. How do you listen to customers to obtain actionable information?
<--- Score

133. Why is application functionality important for you now?
<--- Score

134. What projects are going on in the organization today, and what resources are those projects using from the resource pools?
<--- Score

135. Who is the main stakeholder, with ultimate responsibility for driving application functionality forward?
<--- Score

136. How do you maintain application functionality's Integrity?
<--- Score

137. Who is responsible for errors?
<--- Score

138. Who are your customers?
<--- Score

139. What application functionality modifications can you make work for you?
<--- Score

140. If you find that you havent accomplished one of the goals for one of the steps of the application functionality strategy, what will you do to fix it?
<--- Score

141. How do you set application functionality stretch targets and how do you get people to not only participate in setting these stretch targets but also that they strive to achieve these?
<--- Score

142. If you were responsible for initiating and implementing major changes in your organization, what steps might you take to ensure acceptance of those changes?
<--- Score

143. What goals did you miss?
<--- Score

144. Why do and why don't your customers like your organization?
<--- Score

145. Which application functionality goals are the most important?
<--- Score

146. What trouble can you get into?
<--- Score

147. How do you decide how much to remunerate an employee?
<--- Score

148. How do you govern and fulfill your societal responsibilities?
<--- Score

149. Who else should you help?

<--- Score

150. Can you maintain your growth without detracting from the factors that have contributed to your success?
<--- Score

151. Do you say no to customers for no reason?
<--- Score

152. Will there be any necessary staff changes (redundancies or new hires)?
<--- Score

153. What is something you believe that nearly no one agrees with you on?
<--- Score

154. Who do you want your customers to become?
<--- Score

155. How will you know that the application functionality project has been successful?
<--- Score

156. What is it like to work for you?
<--- Score

157. To whom do you add value?
<--- Score

158. Do you have past application functionality successes?
<--- Score

159. Why is it important to have senior management

support for a application functionality project?
<--- Score

160. In a project to restructure application functionality outcomes, which stakeholders would you involve?
<--- Score

161. How do you manage application functionality Knowledge Management (KM)?
<--- Score

162. Do you think application functionality accomplishes the goals you expect it to accomplish?
<--- Score

163. What are internal and external application functionality relations?
<--- Score

164. Do you feel that more should be done in the application functionality area?
<--- Score

165. How do you stay inspired?
<--- Score

166. Who is responsible for ensuring appropriate resources (time, people and money) are allocated to application functionality?
<--- Score

167. How do you track customer value, profitability or financial return, organizational success, and sustainability?
<--- Score

168. If your customer were your grandmother, would you tell her to buy what you're selling?

<--- Score

169. Which functions and people interact with the supplier and or customer?

<--- Score

170. When information truly is ubiquitous, when reach and connectivity are completely global, when computing resources are infinite, and when a whole new set of impossibilities are not only possible, but happening, what will that do to your business?

<--- Score

171. How can you become more high-tech but still be high touch?

<--- Score

172. If your company went out of business tomorrow, would anyone who doesn't get a paycheck here care?

<--- Score

173. What knowledge, skills and characteristics mark a good application functionality project manager?

<--- Score

174. What are strategies for increasing support and reducing opposition?

<--- Score

175. What is your question? Why?

<--- Score

176. What are the rules and assumptions your industry operates under? What if the opposite were true?
<--- Score

177. Where can you break convention?
<--- Score

178. What unique value proposition (UVP) do you offer?
<--- Score

179. What is your formula for success in application functionality ?
<--- Score

180. How do you foster the skills, knowledge, talents, attributes, and characteristics you want to have?
<--- Score

181. How can you incorporate support to ensure safe and effective use of application functionality into the services that you provide?
<--- Score

182. What is the range of capabilities?
<--- Score

183. Are assumptions made in application functionality stated explicitly?
<--- Score

184. How likely is it that a customer would recommend your company to a friend or colleague?
<--- Score

185. What are the long-term application functionality goals?

<--- Score

186. Is maximizing application functionality protection the same as minimizing application functionality loss?

<--- Score

187. In retrospect, of the projects that you pulled the plug on, what percent do you wish had been allowed to keep going, and what percent do you wish had ended earlier?

<--- Score

188. What are specific application functionality rules to follow?

<--- Score

189. What is the kind of project structure that would be appropriate for your application functionality project, should it be formal and complex, or can it be less formal and relatively simple?

<--- Score

190. How do you determine the key elements that affect application functionality workforce satisfaction, how are these elements determined for different workforce groups and segments?

<--- Score

191. What are the potential basics of application functionality fraud?

<--- Score

Add up total points for this section:

_____ = Total points for this section

Divided by: _____ (number of
statements answered) = _____
Average score for this section

Transfer your score to the application
functionality Index at the beginning of
the Self-Assessment.

Application Functionality and Managing Projects, Criteria for Project Managers:

1.0 Initiating Process Group: Application Functionality

1. When must it be done?

2. Professionals want to know what is expected from them what are the deliverables?

3. Realistic - are the desired results expressed in a way that the team will be motivated and believe that the required level of involvement will be obtained?

4. Did the Application Functionality project team have the right skills?

5. What is the NEXT thing to do?

6. What are the overarching issues of your organization?

7. What will be the pressing issues of tomorrow?

8. At which stage, in a typical Application Functionality project do stake holders have maximum influence?

9. What are the tools and techniques to be used in each phase?

10. How to control and approve each phase?

11. Who is behind the Application Functionality project?

12. Were decisions made in a timely manner?

13. Who does what?

14. Which of six sigmas dmaic phases focuses on the measurement of internal process that affect factors that are critical to quality?

15. Are you certain deliverables are properly completed and meet quality standards?

16. What are the required resources?

17. What are the pressing issues of the hour?

18. At which cmmi level are software processes documented, standardized, and integrated into a standard to-be practiced process for your organization?

19. Do you understand the quality and control criteria that must be achieved for successful Application Functionality project completion?

20. What are the constraints?

1.1 Project Charter: Application Functionality

21. Fit with other Products Compliments – Cannibalizes?

22. Must Have?

23. What metrics could you look at?

24. What are you striving to accomplish (measurable goal(s))?

25. Assumptions and constraints: what assumptions were made in defining the Application Functionality project?

26. Why do you manage integration?

27. What are the assumptions?

28. What are the deliverables?

29. Strategic fit: what is the strategic initiative identifier for this Application Functionality project?

30. What are you trying to accomplish?

31. Name and describe the elements that deal with providing the detail?

32. Will this replace an existing product?

33. Avoid costs, improve service, and/ or comply with a mandate?

34. What date will the task finish?

35. How will you know a change is an improvement?

36. Application Functionality project background: what is the primary motivation for this Application Functionality project?

37. Who will take notes, document decisions?

38. Who are the stakeholders?

39. How are Application Functionality projects different from operations?

1.2 Stakeholder Register: Application Functionality

40. What are the major Application Functionality project milestones requiring communications or providing communications opportunities?

41. Is your organization ready for change?

42. What & Why?

43. How big is the gap?

44. Who wants to talk about Security?

45. Who is managing stakeholder engagement?

46. What is the power of the stakeholder?

47. How much influence do they have on the Application Functionality project?

48. How will reports be created?

49. How should employers make voices heard?

50. What opportunities exist to provide communications?

1.3 Stakeholder Analysis Matrix: Application Functionality

51. Who will obstruct/hinder the Application Functionality project if they are not involved?

52. Inoculations or payment to receive them?

53. Competitors vulnerabilities?

54. What do your organizations stakeholders do better than anyone else?

55. Are they likely to influence the success or failure of your Application Functionality project?

56. What are the key services, contractual arrangements, or other relationships between stakeholder groups?

57. How much do resources cost?

58. Which conditions out of the control of the management are crucial for the achievement of the immediate objective?

59. Cashflow, start-up cash-drain?

60. What actions can be taken to reduce or mitigate risk?

61. How do they affect the Application Functionality project and its outcomes?

62. Why is it important to identify them?

63. Sustaining internal capabilities?

64. What can the stakeholder prevent from happening?

65. What makes a person a stakeholder?

66. Does the stakeholder want to be involved or merely need to be informed about the Application Functionality project and its process?

67. What is the relationship among stakeholders?

68. Benefit to whom?

69. What obstacles does your organization face?

70. Philosophy and values?

2.0 Planning Process Group: Application Functionality

71. If a risk event occurs, what will you do?

72. How does activity resource estimation affect activity duration estimation?

73. How will you know you did it?

74. What types of differentiated effects are resulting from the Application Functionality project and to what extent?

75. Are you just doing busywork to pass the time?

76. How are the principles of aid effectiveness (ownership, alignment, management for development results and mutual responsibility) being applied in the Application Functionality project?

77. Contingency planning. if a risk event occurs, what will you do?

78. To what extent is the program helping to influence your organizations policy framework?

79. How will you do it?

80. In what ways can the governance of the Application Functionality project be improved so that it has greater likelihood of achieving future sustainability?

81. If action is called for, what form should it take?

82. First of all, should any action be taken?

83. What should you do next?

84. How will users learn how to use the deliverables?

85. How many days can task X be late in starting without affecting the Application Functionality project completion date?

86. What type of estimation method are you using?

87. How well will the chosen processes produce the expected results?

88. Is the schedule for the set products being met?

89. Are work methodologies, financial instruments, etc. shared among departments, organizations and Application Functionality projects?

2.1 Project Management Plan: Application Functionality

90. Do the proposed changes from the Application Functionality project include any significant risks to safety?

91. What does management expect of PMs?

92. What worked well?

93. Did the planning effort collaborate to develop solutions that integrate expertise, policies, programs, and Application Functionality projects across entities?

94. Development trends and opportunities. What if the positive direction and vision of your organization causes expected trends to change?

95. What would you do differently?

96. Are comparable cost estimates used for comparing, screening and selecting alternative plans, and has a reasonable cost estimate been developed for the recommended plan?

97. What if, for example, the positive direction and vision of your organization causes expected trends to change resulting in greater need than expected?

98. Is the budget realistic?

99. Are alternatives safe, functional, constructible,

economical, reasonable and sustainable?

100. Is mitigation authorized or recommended?

101. Was the peer (technical) review of the cost estimates duly coordinated with the cost estimate center of expertise and addressed in the review documentation and certification?

102. Are the proposed Application Functionality project purposes different than a previously authorized Application Functionality project?

103. What data/reports/tools/etc. do program managers need?

104. If the Application Functionality project is complex or scope is specialized, do you have appropriate and/or qualified staff available to perform the tasks?

105. Who manages integration?

106. How do you organize the costs in the Application Functionality project management plan?

107. Is the appropriate plan selected based on your organizations objectives and evaluation criteria expressed in Principles and Guidelines policies?

108. Does the selected plan protect privacy?

2.2 Scope Management Plan: Application Functionality

109. Has the budget been baselined?

110. Have the procedures for identifying variances from estimates & adjusting the detailed work program been followed?

111. Are the proposed Application Functionality project purposes different than the previously authorized Application Functionality project?

112. Have all team members been part of identifying risks?

113. Is documentation created for communication with the suppliers and Vendors?

114. Are post milestone Application Functionality project reviews (PMPR) conducted with your organization at least once a year?

115. To whom will the deliverables be first presented for inspection and verification?

116. Is the Application Functionality project sponsor clearly communicating the business case or rationale for why this Application Functionality project is needed?

117. Time estimation – how much time will be needed?

118. Pop quiz – what changed on Application Functionality project scope statement input?

119. Do you keep stake holders informed?

120. Are you meeting with stake holders and team members?

121. What are the risks of not having good inter-organization cooperation on the Application Functionality project?

122. Are software metrics formally captured, analyzed and used as a basis for other Application Functionality project estimates?

123. Have activity relationships and interdependencies within tasks been adequately identified?

124. Has a proper Application Functionality project work location been established that will allow the team to work together with user personnel?

125. Are adequate resources provided for the quality assurance function?

126. Are Application Functionality project contact logs kept up to date?

127. What are the acceptance criteria (process and criteria to be met for key stakeholder acceptance) and who is authorized to sign off?

2.3 Requirements Management Plan: Application Functionality

128. Is requirements work dependent on any other specific Application Functionality project or non-Application Functionality project activities (e.g. funding, approvals, procurement)?

129. Are all the stakeholders ready for the transition into the user community?

130. What performance metrics will be used?

131. Who is responsible for quantifying the Application Functionality project requirements?

132. Are actual resources expenditures versus planned expenditures acceptable?

133. Could inaccurate or incomplete requirements in this Application Functionality project create a serious risk for the business?

134. Will you perform a Requirements Risk assessment and develop a plan to deal with risks?

135. Do you expect stakeholders to be cooperative?

136. In case of software development; Should you have a test for each code module?

137. How knowledgeable is the team in the proposed application area?

138. Will the contractors involved take full responsibility?

139. Is infrastructure setup part of your Application Functionality project?

140. How knowledgeable is the primary Stakeholder(s) in the proposed application area?

141. Will you document changes to requirements?

142. Is the user satisfied?

143. The wbs is developed as part of a joint planning session. and how do you know that youhave done this right?

144. Who came up with this requirement?

145. Have stakeholders been instructed in the Change Control process?

146. Are actual resource expenditures versus planned still acceptable?

147. How will you develop the schedule of requirements activities?

2.4 Requirements Documentation: Application Functionality

148. What is the risk associated with cost and schedule?

149. How linear / iterative is your Requirements Gathering process (or will it be)?

150. Are there legal issues?

151. The problem with gathering requirements is right there in the word gathering. What images does it conjure?

152. How to document system requirements?

153. What can tools do for us?

154. What marketing channels do you want to use: e-mail, letter or sms?

155. Verifiability. can the requirements be checked?

156. Have the benefits identified with the system being identified clearly?

157. Do technical resources exist?

158. Does the system provide the functions which best support the customers needs?

159. Who is interacting with the system?

160. Are there any requirements conflicts?

161. What will be the integration problems?

162. What is your Elevator Speech?

163. How do you get the user to tell you what they want?

164. What is effective documentation?

165. Completeness. are all functions required by the customer included?

166. Validity. does the system provide the functions which best support the customers needs?

167. What is a show stopper in the requirements?

2.5 Requirements Traceability Matrix: Application Functionality

168. Why use a WBS?

169. How will it affect the stakeholders personally in career?

170. What percentage of Application Functionality projects are producing traceability matrices between requirements and other work products?

171. Will you use a Requirements Traceability Matrix?

172. Is there a requirements traceability process in place?

173. Describe the process for approving requirements so they can be added to the traceability matrix and Application Functionality project work can be performed. Will the Application Functionality project requirements become approved in writing?

174. How small is small enough?

175. How do you manage scope?

176. What are the chronologies, contingencies, consequences, criteria?

177. What is the WBS?

178. Do you have a clear understanding of all

subcontracts in place?

179. Why do you manage scope?

2.6 Project Scope Statement: Application Functionality

180. Once its defined, what is the stability of the Application Functionality project scope?

181. Are the input requirements from the team members clearly documented and communicated?

182. Did your Application Functionality project ask for this?

183. Is the change control process documented and on file?

184. What are the major deliverables of the Application Functionality project?

185. Is the Application Functionality project organization documented and on file?

186. Is the Application Functionality project sponsor function identified and defined?

187. Application Functionality project lead, team lead, solution architect?

188. Were key Application Functionality project stakeholders brought into the Application Functionality project Plan?

189. Is there a process (test plans, inspections, reviews) defined for verifying outputs for each task?

190. Is the plan under configuration management?

191. Will the Application Functionality project risks be managed according to the Application Functionality projects risk management process?

192. What is a process you might recommend to verify the accuracy of the research deliverable?

193. Are there completion/verification criteria defined for each task producing an output?

194. Have the configuration management functions been assigned?

195. What is change?

196. What are the defined meeting materials?

197. Have you been able to thoroughly document the Application Functionality projects assumptions and constraints?

198. Has a method and process for requirement tracking been developed?

2.7 Assumption and Constraint Log: Application Functionality

199. Is staff trained on the software technologies that are being used on the Application Functionality project?

200. Contradictory information between document sections?

201. What strengths do you have?

202. When can log be discarded?

203. What weaknesses do you have?

204. Does the document/deliverable meet general requirements (for example, statement of work) for all deliverables?

205. Can the requirements be traced to the appropriate components of the solution, as well as test scripts?

206. Has the approach and development strategy of the Application Functionality project been defined, documented and accepted by the appropriate stakeholders?

207. Can you perform this task or activity in a more effective manner?

208. Does a documented Application Functionality

project organizational policy & plan (i.e. governance model) exist?

209. Have all necessary approvals been obtained?

210. Is the steering committee active in Application Functionality project oversight?

211. After observing execution of process, is it in compliance with the documented Plan?

212. How many Application Functionality project staff does this specific process affect?

213. What if failure during recovery?

214. Does the traceability documentation describe the tool and/or mechanism to be used to capture traceability throughout the life cycle?

215. What do you log?

216. Would known impacts serve as impediments?

217. What is positive about the current process?

218. Should factors be unpredictable over time?

2.8 Work Breakdown Structure: Application Functionality

219. How far down?

220. How will you and your Application Functionality project team define the Application Functionality projects scope and work breakdown structure?

221. When do you stop?

222. Where does it take place?

223. How big is a work-package?

224. Is it still viable?

225. Do you need another level?

226. Why would you develop a Work Breakdown Structure?

227. How many levels?

228. Is the work breakdown structure (wbs) defined and is the scope of the Application Functionality project clear with assigned deliverable owners?

229. What is the probability that the Application Functionality project duration will exceed xx weeks?

230. When would you develop a Work Breakdown Structure?

231. Who has to do it?

232. What has to be done?

233. How much detail?

234. Why is it useful?

235. Can you make it?

236. When does it have to be done?

2.9 WBS Dictionary: Application Functionality

237. Cwbs elements to be subcontracted, with identification of subcontractors?

238. Are internal budgets for authorized, and not priced changes based on the contractors resource plan for accomplishing the work?

239. Are work packages reasonably short in time duration or do they have adequate objective indicators/milestones to minimize subjectivity of the in process work evaluation?

240. Are significant decision points, constraints, and interfaces identified as key milestones?

241. Are data elements summarized through the functional organizational structure for progressively higher levels of management?

242. What should you drop in order to add something new?

243. Are detailed work packages planned as far in advance as practicable?

244. Are the bases and rates for allocating costs from each indirect pool consistently applied?

245. Is data disseminated to the contractors management timely, accurate, and usable?

246. The anticipated business volume?

247. Are work packages assigned to performing organizations?

248. Are data elements reconcilable between internal summary reports and reports forwarded to us?

249. Contemplated overhead expenditure for each period based on the best information currently available?

250. All cwbs elements specified for external reporting?

251. Are management actions taken to reduce indirect costs when there are significant adverse variances?

252. Are the responsibilities and authorities of each of the above organizational elements or managers clearly defined?

253. Are indirect costs charged to the appropriate indirect pools and incurring organization?

254. Contractor financial periods; for example, annual?

255. Is subcontracted work defined and identified to the appropriate subcontractor within the proper WBS element?

256. Are estimates of costs at completion generated in a rational, consistent manner?

2.10 Schedule Management Plan: Application Functionality

257. Have Application Functionality project management standards and procedures been identified / established and documented?

258. Is the schedule vertically and horizontally traceable?

259. Does the business case include how the Application Functionality project aligns with your organizations strategic goals & objectives?

260. Are schedule performance measures defined including pre-set triggers for specific actions?

261. Is your organization certified as a supplier, wholesaler and/or regular dealer?

262. Who is responsible for estimating the activity resources?

263. Are all payments made according to the contract(s)?

264. Are all key components of a Quality Assurance Plan present?

265. Is there an onboarding process in place?

266. Were Application Functionality project team members involved in the development of activity &

task decomposition?

267. Are all vendor contracts closed out?

268. Which status reports are received per the Application Functionality project Plan?

269. Why conduct schedule analysis?

270. Are scheduled deliverables actually delivered?

271. Is there anything planned that does not need to be here?

272. Are written status reports provided on a designated frequent basis?

273. Is your organization certified as a broker of the products/supplies?

274. Is there a set of procedures defining the scope, procedures, and deliverables defining quality control?

275. Have all involved Application Functionality project stakeholders and work groups committed to the Application Functionality project?

2.11 Activity List: Application Functionality

276. When will the work be performed?

277. What is your organizations history in doing similar activities?

278. How can the Application Functionality project be displayed graphically to better visualize the activities?

279. What did not go as well?

280. How do you determine the late start (LS) for each activity?

281. For other activities, how much delay can be tolerated?

282. Are the required resources available or need to be acquired?

283. How difficult will it be to do specific activities on this Application Functionality project?

284. How detailed should a Application Functionality project get?

285. Is infrastructure setup part of your Application Functionality project?

286. What are the critical bottleneck activities?

287. How should ongoing costs be monitored to try to keep the Application Functionality project within budget?

288. What went well?

289. Should you include sub-activities?

290. Where will it be performed?

291. What is the total time required to complete the Application Functionality project if no delays occur?

292. Who will perform the work?

293. What will be performed?

2.12 Activity Attributes: Application Functionality

294. Does your organization of the data change its meaning?

295. Have you identified the Activity Leveling Priority code value on each activity?

296. Were there other ways you could have organized the data to achieve similar results?

297. How else could the items be grouped?

298. Why?

299. Have constraints been applied to the start and finish milestones for the phases?

300. How many resources do you need to complete the work scope within a limit of X number of days?

301. How much activity detail is required?

302. Would you consider either of corresponding activities an outlier?

303. How difficult will it be to do specific activities on this Application Functionality project?

304. What went right?

305. What went wrong?

306. Is there a trend during the year?

307. What is missing?

308. Where else does it apply?

309. Activity: what is Missing?

310. Activity: what is In the Bag?

2.13 Milestone List: Application Functionality

311. Effects on core activities, distraction?

312. How late can the activity finish?

313. Do you foresee any technical risks or developmental challenges?

314. What are your competitors vulnerabilities?

315. Marketing - reach, distribution, awareness?

316. Legislative effects?

317. Environmental effects?

318. What has been done so far?

319. How will you get the word out to customers?

320. What specific improvements did you make to the Application Functionality project proposal since the previous time?

321. Reliability of data, plan predictability?

322. New USPs?

323. Own known vulnerabilities?

324. Describe the industry you are in and the market

growth opportunities. What is the market for your technology, product or service?

325. How do you manage time?

326. How will the milestone be verified?

327. Gaps in capabilities?

328. Who will manage the Application Functionality project on a day-to-day basis?

2.14 Network Diagram: Application Functionality

329. If the Application Functionality project network diagram cannot change and you have extra personnel resources, what is the BEST thing to do?

330. Can you calculate the confidence level?

331. What are the tools?

332. What controls the start and finish of a job?

333. Which type of network diagram allows you to depict four types of dependencies?

334. What are the Key Success Factors?

335. What activities must occur simultaneously with this activity?

336. Planning: who, how long, what to do?

337. Review the logical flow of the network diagram. Take a look at which activities you have first and then sequence the activities. Do they make sense?

338. Will crashing x weeks return more in benefits than it costs?

339. What activities must follow this activity?

340. What job or jobs follow it?

341. What activity must be completed immediately before this activity can start?

342. Are you on time?

343. How confident can you be in your milestone dates and the delivery date?

344. Where do you schedule uncertainty time?

345. What to do and When?

346. What job or jobs could run concurrently?

347. What is the completion time?

348. What are the Major Administrative Issues?

2.15 Activity Resource Requirements: Application Functionality

349. Organizational Applicability?

350. Anything else?

351. How do you handle petty cash?

352. Other support in specific areas?

353. What is the Work Plan Standard?

354. How many signatures do you require on a check and does this match what is in your policy and procedures?

355. Why do you do that?

356. When does monitoring begin?

357. What are constraints that you might find during the Human Resource Planning process?

358. Which logical relationship does the PDM use most often?

359. Are there unresolved issues that need to be addressed?

360. Time for overtime?

361. Do you use tools like decomposition and rolling-

wave planning to produce the activity list and other outputs?

2.16 Resource Breakdown Structure: Application Functionality

362. What is Application Functionality project communication management?

363. How can this help you with team building?

364. Who will use the system?

365. How difficult will it be to do specific activities on this Application Functionality project?

366. Goals for the Application Functionality project. What is each stakeholders desired outcome for the Application Functionality project?

367. Who needs what information?

368. What defines a successful Application Functionality project?

369. How should the information be delivered?

370. Why is this important?

371. Any changes from stakeholders?

372. What is the number one predictor of a groups productivity?

373. What is each stakeholders desired outcome for the Application Functionality project?

374. Which resources should be in the resource pool?

375. Who will be used as a Application Functionality project team member?

376. Who is allowed to see what data about which resources?

377. Who is allowed to perform which functions?

378. Which resource planning tool provides information on resource responsibility and accountability?

2.17 Activity Duration Estimates: Application Functionality

379. Is earned value analysis completed to assess Application Functionality project performance?

380. What is involved in the solicitation process?

381. What questions do you have about the sample documents provided?

382. What are the largest companies that provide information technology outsourcing services?

383. Does a process exist to identify individuals authorized to make certain decisions?

384. Is the work performed reviewed against contractual objectives?

385. Are performance reviews conducted regularly to assess the status of Application Functionality projects?

386. Will new hardware or software be required for servers or client machines?

387. Will the new application negatively affect the current IT infrastructure?

388. Calculate the expected duration for an activity that has a most likely time of 3, a pessimistic time of 10, and a optimiztic time of 2?

389. What type of people would you want on your team?

390. Do an internet search on earning pmp certification. be sure to search for yahoo groups related to this topic. what are the options you found to help people prepare for the exam?

391. Does a process exist for approving or rejecting changes?

392. Do they make sense?

393. What tasks must follow this task?

394. Given your research into similar classes and the work you think is required for this Application Functionality project, what assumptions, variables, or costs would you change from the information provided above?

395. What do you think the real problem was in this case?

396. Does a process exist to identify Application Functionality project roles, responsibilities and reporting relationships?

397. Are activity duration estimates documented?

2.18 Duration Estimating Worksheet: Application Functionality

398. Is a construction detail attached (to aid in explanation)?

399. Is this operation cost effective?

400. Value pocket identification & quantification what are value pockets?

401. When do the individual activities need to start and finish?

402. What is next?

403. Define the work as completely as possible. What work will be included in the Application Functionality project?

404. What is an Average Application Functionality project?

405. Science = process: remember the scientific method?

406. What utility impacts are there?

407. Can the Application Functionality project be constructed as planned?

408. Why estimate costs?

409. Do any colleagues have experience with your organization and/or RFPs?

410. What is the total time required to complete the Application Functionality project if no delays occur?

411. What work will be included in the Application Functionality project?

412. Is the Application Functionality project responsive to community need?

413. What questions do you have?

2.19 Project Schedule: Application Functionality

414. Schedule/cost recovery?

415. Meet requirements?

416. How closely did the initial Application Functionality project Schedule compare with the actual schedule?

417. How effectively were issues able to be resolved without impacting the Application Functionality project Schedule or Budget?

418. What is the purpose of a Application Functionality project schedule?

419. What is the most mis-scheduled part of process?

420. How do you know that youhave done this right?

421. What is Application Functionality project management?

422. Are quality inspections and review activities listed in the Application Functionality project schedule(s)?

423. Eliminate unnecessary activities. Are there activities that came from a template or previous Application Functionality project that are not applicable on this phase of this Application

Functionality project?

424. Are the original Application Functionality project schedule and budget realistic?

425. Your Application Functionality project management plan results in a Application Functionality project schedule that is too long. If the Application Functionality project network diagram cannot change and you have extra personnel resources, what is the BEST thing to do?

426. How detailed should a Application Functionality project get?

427. Why or why not?

428. How does a Application Functionality project get to be a year late ?

429. Master Application Functionality project schedule?

430. How can you minimize or control changes to Application Functionality project schedules?

2.20 Cost Management Plan: Application Functionality

431. Are the Application Functionality project plans updated on a frequent basis?

432. Is the schedule updated on a periodic basis?

433. Are changes in deliverable commitments agreed to by all affected groups & individuals?

434. Are staff skills known and available for each task?

435. Are internal Application Functionality project status meetings held at reasonable intervals?

436. Resources – how will human resources be scheduled during each phase of the Application Functionality project?

437. Are corrective actions and variances reported?

438. Is a pmo (Application Functionality project management office) in place and provide oversight to the Application Functionality project?

439. What threats might prevent you from getting there?

440. What is an Acceptance Management Process?

441. Are status reports received per the Application Functionality project Plan?

442. Are the schedule estimates reasonable given the Application Functionality project?

443. Is there a formal set of procedures supporting Issues Management?

444. Similar Application Functionality projects?

445. Does a documented Application Functionality project organizational policy & plan (i.e. governance model) exist?

446. What is the work breakdown structure for the Application Functionality project?

2.21 Activity Cost Estimates: Application Functionality

447. How quickly can the task be done with the skills available?

448. How do you manage cost?

449. What is the activity inventory?

450. What happens if you cannot produce the documentation for the single audit?

451. Why do you manage cost?

452. What is the last item a Application Functionality project manager must do to finalize Application Functionality project close-out?

453. Based on your Application Functionality project communication management plan, what worked well?

454. How do you change activities?

455. Certification of actual expenditures?

456. Will you need to provide essential services information about activities?

457. Does the activity rely on a common set of tools to carry it out?

458. How many activities should you have?

459. Were you satisfied with the work?

460. Does the activity use a common approach or business function to deliver its results?

461. How and when do you enter into Application Functionality project Procurement Management?

462. Will you use any tools, such as Application Functionality project management software, to assist in capturing Earned Value metrics?

463. How difficult will it be to do specific tasks on the Application Functionality project?

464. What makes a good activity description?

465. Were sponsors and decision makers available when needed outside regularly scheduled meetings?

466. Does the activity serve a common type of customer?

2.22 Cost Estimating Worksheet: Application Functionality

467. Identify the timeframe necessary to monitor progress and collect data to determine how the selected measure has changed?

468. Will the Application Functionality project collaborate with the local community and leverage resources?

469. What costs are to be estimated?

470. What is the purpose of estimating?

471. What additional Application Functionality project(s) could be initiated as a result of this Application Functionality project?

472. Who is best positioned to know and assist in identifying corresponding factors?

473. Can a trend be established from historical performance data on the selected measure and are the criteria for using trend analysis or forecasting methods met?

474. Is it feasible to establish a control group arrangement?

475. What will others want?

476. Ask: are others positioned to know, are others

credible, and will others cooperate?

477. How will the results be shared and to whom?

478. What happens to any remaining funds not used?

479. Does the Application Functionality project provide innovative ways for stakeholders to overcome obstacles or deliver better outcomes?

480. What can be included?

481. What is the estimated labor cost today based upon this information?

482. Is the Application Functionality project responsive to community need?

483. What info is needed?

2.23 Cost Baseline: Application Functionality

484. Are you meeting with your team regularly?

485. What does a good WBS NOT look like?

486. What is the most important thing to do next to make your Application Functionality project successful?

487. Have the resources used by the Application Functionality project been reassigned to other units or Application Functionality projects?

488. Have all approved changes to the cost baseline been identified and impact on the Application Functionality project documented?

489. Vac -variance at completion, how much over/ under budget do you expect to be?

490. How will cost estimates be used?

491. Application Functionality project goals -should others be reconsidered?

492. How difficult will it be to do specific tasks on the Application Functionality project?

493. Verify business objectives. Are others appropriate, and well-articulated?

494. Are there contingencies or conditions related to the acceptance?

495. Has training and knowledge transfer of the operations organization been completed?

496. Have all the product or service deliverables been accepted by the customer?

497. Who will use corresponding metrics ?

498. Is there anything you need from upper management in order to be successful?

499. Have you identified skills that are missing from your team?

500. Have the actual milestone completion dates been compared to the approved schedule?

501. Does a process exist for establishing a cost baseline to measure Application Functionality project performance?

2.24 Quality Management Plan: Application Functionality

502. What are the appropriate test methods to be used?

503. What would you gain if you spent time working to improve this process?

504. How does your organization determine the requirements and product/service features important to customers?

505. How long do you retain data?

506. How do senior leaders create and communicate values and performance expectations?

507. Results Available?

508. How is staff trained on the recording of field notes?

509. How does your organization establish and maintain customer relationships?

510. Is it necessary?

511. Do you keep back-up copies of any data?

512. How does your organization perform analyzes to assess overall organizational performance and set priorities?

513. Are formal code reviews conducted?

514. What changes can you make that will result in improvement?

515. What are your organizations current levels and trends for the already stated measures related to customer satisfaction/ dissatisfaction and product/ service performance?

516. Are there procedures in place to effectively manage interdependencies with other Application Functionality projects / systems?

517. With the five whys method, the team considers why the issue being explored occurred. do others then take that initial answer and ask why?

518. Sampling part of task?

519. How do you ensure that your sampling methods and procedures meet your data quality objectives?

520. How does your organization use comparative data and information to improve organizational performance?

521. What are the established criteria that sampling / testing data are compared against?

2.25 Quality Metrics: Application Functionality

522. How exactly do you define when differences exist?

523. Should a modifier be included?

524. Where is quality now?

525. What group is empowered to define quality requirements?

526. Which are the right metrics to use?

527. What is the CMS Benchmark?

528. What level of statistical confidence do you use?

529. What percentage are outcome-based?

530. How are requirements conflicts resolved?

531. Can you correlate your quality metrics to profitability?

532. How effective are your security tests?

533. Which report did you use to create the data you are submitting?

534. Have alternatives been defined in the event that failure occurs?

535. Has it met internal or external standards?

536. Why is now the time for quality metrics?

537. Are quality metrics defined?

538. What documentation is required?

539. Subjective quality component: customer satisfaction, how do you measure it?

540. Who notifies stakeholders of normal and abnormal results?

2.26 Process Improvement Plan: Application Functionality

541. Management commitment at all levels?

542. What is the return on investment?

543. What personnel are the coaches for your initiative?

544. Are you making progress on the goals?

545. What actions are needed to address the problems and achieve the goals?

546. Where do you want to be?

547. The motive is determined by asking, Why do you want to achieve this goal?

548. Are you following the quality standards?

549. What lessons have you learned so far?

550. Does your process ensure quality?

551. Why do you want to achieve the goal?

552. Why quality management?

553. What personnel are the sponsors for that initiative?

554. What is the test-cycle concept?

555. What is quality and how will you ensure it?

556. Are you making progress on the improvement framework?

557. How do you measure?

558. Does explicit definition of the measures exist?

2.27 Responsibility Assignment Matrix: Application Functionality

559. Not any rs, as, or cs: if an identified role is only informed, should others be eliminated from the matrix?

560. Budgeted cost for work performed?

561. Do all the identified groups or people really need to be consulted?

562. Major functional areas of contract effort?

563. Who is going to do that work?

564. What do people write/say on status/Application Functionality project reports?

565. The already stated responsible for the establishment of budgets and assignment of resources for overhead performance?

566. Time-phased control account budgets?

567. Are all elements of indirect expense identified to overhead cost budgets of Application Functionality projections?

568. Do you know how your people are allocated?

569. Identify potential or actual budget-based and time-based schedule variances?

570. What do you do when people do not respond?

571. Budgets assigned to major functional organizations?

572. Wbs elements contractually specified for reporting of status (lowest level only)?

573. Application Functionality projected economic escalation?

2.28 Roles and Responsibilities: Application Functionality

574. What expectations were met?

575. What should you highlight for improvement?

576. Are your policies supportive of a culture of quality data?

577. What should you do now to prepare yourself for a promotion, increased responsibilities or a different job?

578. Is feedback clearly communicated and non-judgmental?

579. Was the expectation clearly communicated?

580. Are the quality assurance functions and related roles and responsibilities clearly defined?

581. Once the responsibilities are defined for the Application Functionality project, have the deliverables, roles and responsibilities been clearly communicated to every participant?

582. Does your vision/mission support a culture of quality data?

583. Implementation of actions: Who are the responsible units?

584. How is your work-life balance?

585. To decide whether to use a quality measurement, ask how will you know when it is achieved?

586. Required skills, knowledge, experience?

587. Does the team have access to and ability to use data analysis tools?

588. Be specific; avoid generalities. Thank you and great work alone are insufficient. What exactly do you appreciate and why?

589. Who is responsible for each task?

590. Who is involved?

591. What expectations were NOT met?

592. What areas would you highlight for changes or improvements?

2.29 Human Resource Management Plan: Application Functionality

593. Were escalated issues resolved promptly?

594. How are superior performers differentiated from average performers?

595. What are the Staffing Requirements?

596. Where is your organization headed?

597. Have lessons learned been conducted after each Application Functionality project release?

598. Have Application Functionality project management standards and procedures been identified / established and documented?

599. Is there a set of procedures to capture, analyze and act on quality metrics?

600. Quality assurance overheads?

601. Is your organization human?

602. How complete is the human resource management plan?

603. Do Application Functionality project managers participating in the Application Functionality project know the Application Functionality projects true status first hand?

604. Personnel with expertise?

605. Are meeting objectives identified for each meeting?

606. Are multiple estimation methods being employed?

607. Are the quality tools and methods identified in the Quality Plan appropriate to the Application Functionality project?

608. Is Application Functionality project status reviewed with the steering and executive teams at appropriate intervals?

609. Were the budget estimates reasonable?

610. Are updated Application Functionality project time & resource estimates reasonable based on the current Application Functionality project stage?

611. Is there an on-going process in place to monitor Application Functionality project risks?

2.30 Communications Management Plan: Application Functionality

612. What does the stakeholder need from the team?

613. Why manage stakeholders?

614. How much time does it take to do it?

615. Which stakeholders are thought leaders, influences, or early adopters?

616. Are there potential barriers between the team and the stakeholder?

617. How often do you engage with stakeholders?

618. What help do you and your team need from the stakeholder?

619. Who are the members of the governing body?

620. Why is stakeholder engagement important?

621. In your work, how much time is spent on stakeholder identification?

622. Do you have members of your team responsible for certain stakeholders?

623. Who is the stakeholder?

624. Are the stakeholders getting the information

others need, are others consulted, are concerns addressed?

625. Who is responsible?

626. What to learn?

627. Where do team members get information?

628. How will the person responsible for executing the communication item be notified?

629. Are there common objectives between the team and the stakeholder?

630. What communications method?

2.31 Risk Management Plan: Application Functionality

631. Which risks should get the attention?

632. Management -what contingency plans do you have if the risk becomes a reality?

633. Is the customer willing to commit significant time to the requirements gathering process?

634. Are you working on the right risks?

635. Are the software tools integrated with each other?

636. Are enough people available?

637. What is the cost to the Application Functionality project if it does occur?

638. Market risk: will the new product be useful to your organization or marketable to others?

639. Have you worked with the customer in the past?

640. Is the number of people on the Application Functionality project team adequate to do the job?

641. Has something like this been done before?

642. Are the metrics meaningful and useful?

643. What things might go wrong?

644. Anticipated volatility of the requirements?

645. Risk may be made during which step of risk management?

646. How are risk analvsis and prioritization performed?

647. Is the customer willing to participate in reviews?

648. Methodology: how will risk management be performed on this Application Functionality project?

649. Do the requirements require the creation of components that are unlike anything your organization has previously built?

650. Why is product liability a serious issue?

2.32 Risk Register: Application Functionality

651. Schedule impact/severity estimated range (workdays) assume the event happens, what is the potential impact?

652. User involvement: do you have the right users?

653. What should you do now?

654. Budget and schedule: what are the estimated costs and schedules for performing risk-related activities?

655. What is the reason for current performance gaps and do the risks and opportunities identified previously account for this?

656. How are risks identified?

657. Preventative actions - planned actions to reduce the likelihood a risk will occur and/or reduce the seriousness should it occur. What should you do now?

658. What are you going to do to limit the Application Functionality projects risk exposure due to the identified risks?

659. What are the main aims, objectives of the policy, strategy, or service and the intended outcomes?

660. Are there any knock-on effects/impact on any of

the other areas?

661. What further options might be available for responding to the risk?

662. What is the probability and impact of the risk occurring?

663. Manageability – have mitigations to the risk been identified?

664. What are your key risks/show istoppers and what is being done to manage them?

665. What would the impact to the Application Functionality project objectives be should the risk arise?

666. What action, if any, has been taken to respond to the risk?

667. Methodology: how will risk management be performed on this Application Functionality project?

668. Are there other alternative controls that could be implemented?

669. How is a Community Risk Register created?

670. Cost/benefit – how much will the proposed mitigations cost and how does this cost compare with the potential cost of the risk event/situation should it occur?

2.33 Probability and Impact Assessment: Application Functionality

671. Who has experience with this?

672. Do the requirements require the creation of new algorithms?

673. How will the consumption pattern change?

674. What things are likely to change?

675. Are some people working on multiple Application Functionality projects?

676. My Application Functionality project leader has suddenly left your organization, what do you do?

677. What are the chances the event will occur?

678. Would avoiding any of corresponding impact the Application Functionality projects chance of success?

679. Can it be enlarged by drawing people from other areas of your organization?

680. How completely has the customer been identified?

681. Can you stabilize dynamic risk factors?

682. What should be the gestation period for the

Application Functionality project with specific technology?

683. How are you working with risks?

684. How risk averse are you?

685. What are the risks involved in appointing external agencies to manage the Application Functionality project?

686. What are the probabilities of chosen technologies being suitable for local conditions?

687. Are end-users enthusiastically committed to the Application Functionality project and the system/product to be built?

688. When and how will the recent breakthroughs in basic research lead to commercial products?

689. Do you use diagramming techniques to show cause and effect?

2.34 Probability and Impact Matrix: Application Functionality

690. Do end-users have realistic expectations?

691. What can you use the analyzed risks for?

692. What is the likelihood?

693. What do you expect?

694. What new technologies are being explored in the same area?

695. What is the risk appetite?

696. Lay ground work for future returns?

697. How carefully have the potential competitors been identified?

698. Can it be changed quickly?

699. Do others match with the clients requirement?

700. Has the need for the Application Functionality project been properly established?

701. How are risks and risk management perceived in the Application Functionality project?

702. What changes in the regulation are forthcoming?

703. Non-valid or incredible information?

704. Do you need a risk management plan?

705. What will be the environmental impact of the Application Functionality project?

706. How solid is the Application Functionality projection of competitive reaction?

707. What can you do about it?

708. Which should be probably done NEXT?

2.35 Risk Data Sheet: Application Functionality

709. Do effective diagnostic tests exist?

710. What can you do?

711. What actions can be taken to eliminate or remove risk?

712. How can it happen?

713. What are the main opportunities available to you that you should grab while you can?

714. What do you know?

715. Who has a vested interest in how you perform as your organization (our stakeholders)?

716. What are the main threats to your existence?

717. If it happens, what are the consequences?

718. Has a sensitivity analysis been carried out?

719. What are you trying to achieve (Objectives)?

720. How reliable is the data source?

721. How do you handle product safely?

722. What are your core values?

723. What are you here for (Mission)?

724. Potential for recurrence?

725. What were the Causes that contributed?

726. How can hazards be reduced?

727. Are new hazards created?

2.36 Procurement Management Plan: Application Functionality

728. Do you have the reasons why the changes to your organizational systems and capabilities are required?

729. Are Application Functionality project team roles and responsibilities identified and documented?

730. Published materials?

731. Have process improvement efforts been completed before requirements efforts begin?

732. Is there a procurement management plan in place?

733. Are quality inspections and review activities listed in the Application Functionality project schedule(s)?

734. Similar Application Functionality projects?

735. Are the people assigned to the Application Functionality project sufficiently qualified?

736. Have lessons learned been conducted after each Application Functionality project release?

737. Are there checklists created to determine if all quality processes are followed?

738. Have the key elements of a coherent Application Functionality project management strategy been established?

739. Are vendor contract reports, reviews and visits conducted periodically?

740. Is quality monitored from the perspective of the customers needs and expectations?

741. Has a quality assurance plan been developed for the Application Functionality project?

742. Is a pmo (Application Functionality project management office) in place which provides oversight to the Application Functionality project?

743. Has the business need been clearly defined?

744. Are Application Functionality project team members committed fulltime?

2.37 Source Selection Criteria: Application Functionality

745. How and when do you enter into Application Functionality project Procurement Management?

746. Do you have designated specific forms or worksheets?

747. What should communications be used to accomplish?

748. How should the preproposal conference be conducted?

749. How is past performance evaluated?

750. What are the requirements for publicizing a RFP?

751. Is the offeror pricing what is technically proposed?

752. How important is cost in the source selection decision relative to past performance and technical considerations?

753. Do you consider all weaknesses, significant weaknesses, and deficiencies?

754. Do you want to wait until all offerors have been evaluated?

755. What management structure does your

organization consider as optimal for performing the contract?

756. What are open book debriefings?

757. How are oral presentations documented?

758. When is it appropriate to conduct a preproposal conference?

759. When is it appropriate to issue a Draft Request for Proposal (DRFP)?

760. Are there any specific considerations that precludes offers from being selected as the awardee?

761. What does a sample rating scale look like?

762. What are the special considerations for preaward debriefings?

763. What benefits are accrued from issuing a DRFP in advance of issuing a final RFP?

764. What is price analysis and when should it be performed?

2.38 Stakeholder Management Plan: Application Functionality

765. Has a resource management plan been created?

766. Contradictory information between different documents?

767. How are new requirements or changes to requirements identified?

768. What information should be collected?

769. Were Application Functionality project team members involved in the development of activity & task decomposition?

770. Alignment to strategic goals & objectives?

771. Is there a formal process for updating the Application Functionality project baseline?

772. What is the process for purchases that arent acceptable (eg damaged goods)?

773. Do you know what your customers expectations are regarding this process?

774. Have Application Functionality project management standards and procedures been established and documented?

775. What are the procedures and processes to be

followed for purchases, including approval and authorisation requirements?

776. Have adequate resources been provided by management to ensure Application Functionality project success?

777. Where to get additional help?

778. Does the Application Functionality project have a formal Application Functionality project Charter?

779. What is the difference between product and Application Functionality project scope?

780. Why would you develop a Application Functionality project Execution Plan?

781. Are Application Functionality project contact logs kept up to date?

782. Are there standards for code development?

783. Do all stakeholders know how to access this repository and where to find the Application Functionality project documentation?

784. Will all relevant stakeholders be included within the review process?

2.39 Change Management Plan: Application Functionality

785. What provokes organizational change?

786. Who will do the training?

787. Is it the same for each of the business units?

788. Is there support for this application(s) and are the details available for distribution?

789. Readiness -what is a successful end state?

790. Where will the funds come from?

791. Different application of an existing process?

792. What does a resilient organization look like?

793. Will the readiness criteria be met prior to the training roll out?

794. Has the training co-ordinator been provided with the training details and put in place the necessary arrangements?

795. Who is responsible for which tasks?

796. Is there a need for new relationships to be built?

797. Who might be able to help you the most?

798. What did the people around you say about it?

799. Who will fund the training?

800. Is there a software application relevant to this deliverable?

801. What tasks are needed?

802. Identify the current level of skills and knowledge and behaviours of the group that will be impacted on. What prerequisite knowledge do corresponding groups need?

3.0 Executing Process Group: Application Functionality

803. What are deliverables of your Application Functionality project?

804. What is the difference between conceptual, application, and evaluative questions?

805. Will outside resources be needed to help?

806. When will the Application Functionality project be done?

807. How well did the chosen processes produce the expected results?

808. How do you prevent staff are just doing busywork to pass the time?

809. Based on your Application Functionality project communication management plan, what worked well?

810. What are crucial elements of successful Application Functionality project plan execution?

811. What are the main types of goods and services being outsourced?

812. How many different communication channels does the Application Functionality project team have?

813. What is the difference between using brainstorming and the Delphi technique for risk identification?

814. Mitigate. what will you do to minimize the impact should a risk event occur?

815. Does the case present a realistic scenario?

816. What business situation is being addressed?

817. When is the appropriate time to bring the scorecard to Board meetings?

3.1 Team Member Status Report: Application Functionality

818. How will resource planning be done?

819. The problem with Reward & Recognition Programs is that the truly deserving people all too often get left out. How can you make it practical?

820. Are the products of your organizations Application Functionality projects meeting customers objectives?

821. How can you make it practical?

822. What is to be done?

823. Are the attitudes of staff regarding Application Functionality project work improving?

824. Why is it to be done?

825. How does this product, good, or service meet the needs of the Application Functionality project and your organization as a whole?

826. Do you have an Enterprise Application Functionality project Management Office (EPMO)?

827. How much risk is involved?

828. Will the staff do training or is that done by a third party?

829. What specific interest groups do you have in place?

830. Is there evidence that staff is taking a more professional approach toward management of your organizations Application Functionality projects?

831. Does the product, good, or service already exist within your organization?

832. Does every department have to have a Application Functionality project Manager on staff?

833. When a teams productivity and success depend on collaboration and the efficient flow of information, what generally fails them?

834. Are your organizations Application Functionality projects more successful over time?

835. Does your organization have the means (staff, money, contract, etc.) to produce or to acquire the product, good, or service?

836. How it is to be done?

3.2 Change Request: Application Functionality

837. How do you get changes (code) out in a timely manner?

838. What mechanism is used to appraise others of changes that are made?

839. Change request coordination ?

840. How to get changes (code) out in a timely manner?

841. How can you ensure that changes have been made properly?

842. How are the measures for carrying out the change established?

843. Will this change conflict with other requirements changes (e.g., lead to conflicting operational scenarios)?

844. What has an inspector to inspect and to check?

845. Who is communicating the change?

846. How shall the implementation of changes be recorded?

847. Why control change across the life cycle?

848. Why do you want to have a change control system?

849. How do team members communicate with each other?

850. Can static requirements change attributes like the size of the change be used to predict reliability in execution?

851. Have scm procedures for noting the change, recording it, and reporting it been followed?

852. When to submit a change request?

853. Since there are no change requests in your Application Functionality project at this point, what must you have before you begin?

854. Why were your requested changes rejected or not made?

855. What is the purpose of change control?

856. Should staff call into the helpdesk or go to the website?

3.3 Change Log: Application Functionality

857. Is the change request within Application Functionality project scope?

858. When was the request approved?

859. Who initiated the change request?

860. How does this relate to the standards developed for specific business processes?

861. Where do changes come from?

862. Is the submitted change a new change or a modification of a previously approved change?

863. Is this a mandatory replacement?

864. How does this change affect the timeline of the schedule?

865. Is the change request open, closed or pending?

866. Does the suggested change request seem to represent a necessary enhancement to the product?

867. Is the requested change request a result of changes in other Application Functionality project(s)?

868. Does the suggested change request represent a desired enhancement to the products functionality?

869. Do the described changes impact on the integrity or security of the system?

870. Should a more thorough impact analysis be conducted?

871. Will the Application Functionality project fail if the change request is not executed?

872. How does this change affect scope?

873. When was the request submitted?

874. Is the change backward compatible without limitations?

3.4 Decision Log: Application Functionality

875. What eDiscovery problem or issue did your organization set out to fix or make better?

876. What is the line where eDiscovery ends and document review begins?

877. How effective is maintaining the log at facilitating organizational learning?

878. Is everything working as expected?

879. Which variables make a critical difference?

880. What alternatives/risks were considered?

881. Adversarial environment. is your opponent open to a non-traditional workflow, or will it likely challenge anything you do?

882. Does anything need to be adjusted?

883. How does the use a Decision Support System influence the strategies/tactics or costs?

884. Linked to original objective?

885. How do you define success?

886. With whom was the decision shared or considered?

887. Who will be given a copy of this document and where will it be kept?

888. What is your overall strategy for quality control / quality assurance procedures?

889. At what point in time does loss become unacceptable?

890. Is your opponent open to a non-traditional workflow, or will it likely challenge anything you do?

891. How does an increasing emphasis on cost containment influence the strategies and tactics used?

892. What is the average size of your matters in an applicable measurement?

893. It becomes critical to track and periodically revisit both operational effectiveness; Are you noticing all that you need to, and are you interpreting what you see effectively?

894. How consolidated and comprehensive a story can you tell by capturing currently available incident data in a central location and through a log of key decisions during an incident?

3.5 Quality Audit: Application Functionality

895. Is there a written procedure for receiving materials?

896. How does your organization know that its relationships with the community at large are appropriately effective and constructive?

897. How does your organization know that its advisory services are appropriately effective and constructive?

898. How does your organization know that it is effectively and constructively guiding staff through to timely completion of tasks?

899. How does your organization ensure that equipment is appropriately maintained and producing valid results?

900. Is the continuing professional education of key personnel account fored in detail?

901. Are people allowed to contribute ideas?

902. How does your organization know that its relationship with its (past) staff is appropriately effective and constructive?

903. Can your organization demonstrate exactly how and why results were achieved?

904. What are your supplier audits?

905. Does the report read coherently?

906. Are there sufficient personnel having the necessary education, background, training, and experience to assure that all operations are correctly performed?

907. How does your organization know that its staff financial services are appropriately effective and constructive?

908. What is the collective experience of the team to be assigned to an audit?

909. How does your organization know that its system for recruiting the best staff possible are appropriately effective and constructive?

910. Is your organizational structure a help or a hindrance to deployment?

911. What review processes are in place for your organizations major activities?

912. Is your organizational structure established and each positions responsibility defined?

913. Are goals well supported with strategies, operational plans, manuals and training?

3.6 Team Directory: Application Functionality

914. Process decisions: are there any statutory or regulatory issues relevant to the timely execution of work?

915. What are you going to deliver or accomplish?

916. How will you accomplish and manage the objectives?

917. Who are the Team Members?

918. Where will the product be used and/or delivered or built when appropriate?

919. Who are your stakeholders (customers, sponsors, end users, team members)?

920. How do unidentified risks impact the outcome of the Application Functionality project?

921. Who should receive information (all stakeholders)?

922. How does the team resolve conflicts and ensure tasks are completed?

923. Have you decided when to celebrate the Application Functionality projects completion date?

924. Who will talk to the customer?

925. Process decisions: do invoice amounts match accepted work in place?

926. Process decisions: are contractors adequately prosecuting the work?

927. Why is the work necessary?

928. Who will report Application Functionality project status to all stakeholders?

929. Process decisions: is work progressing on schedule and per contract requirements?

930. Process decisions: are all start-up, turn over and close out requirements of the contract satisfied?

931. Does a Application Functionality project team directory list all resources assigned to the Application Functionality project?

3.7 Team Operating Agreement: Application Functionality

932. What is culture?

933. Why does your organization want to participate in teaming?

934. What resources can be provided for the team in terms of equipment, space, time for training, protected time and space for meetings, and travel allowances?

935. What is the number of cases currently teamed?

936. Do you leverage technology engagement tools group chat, polls, screen sharing, etc.?

937. Do you send out the agenda and meeting materials in advance?

938. What administrative supports will be put in place to support the team and the teams supervisor?

939. What is group supervision?

940. Do you use a parking lot for any items that are important and outside of the agenda?

941. Does your team need access to all documents and information at all times?

942. Do you brief absent members after they view

meeting notes or listen to a recording?

943. Do you upload presentation materials in advance and test the technology?

944. Did you determine the technology methods that best match the messages to be communicated?

945. Do team members reside in more than two countries?

946. The method to be used in the decision making process; Will it be consensus, majority rule, or the supervisor having the final say?

947. Do you post any action items, due dates, and responsibilities on the team website?

948. Have you set the goals and objectives of the team?

949. Did you prepare participants for the next meeting?

950. What is teaming?

951. Do you determine the meeting length and time of day?

3.8 Team Performance Assessment: Application Functionality

952. Individual task proficiency and team process behavior: what is important for team functioning?

953. What do you think is the most constructive thing that could be done now to resolve considerations and disputes about method variance?

954. To what degree do members articulate the goals beyond the team membership?

955. If you are worried about method variance before you collect data, what sort of design elements might you include to reduce or eliminate the threat of method variance?

956. How do you encourage members to learn from each other?

957. Lack of method variance in self-reported affect and perceptions at work: Reality or artifact?

958. To what degree is there a sense that only the team can succeed?

959. To what degree can all members engage in open and interactive considerations?

960. To what degree do team members articulate the teams work approach?

961. To what degree does the teams work approach provide opportunity for members to engage in results-based evaluation?

962. If you have received criticism from reviewers that your work suffered from method variance, what was the circumstance?

963. When a reviewer complains about method variance, what is the essence of the complaint?

964. What makes opportunities more or less obvious?

965. How do you recognize and praise members for contributions?

966. To what degree can the team measure progress against specific goals?

967. To what degree can team members meet frequently enough to accomplish the teams ends?

968. To what degree do all members feel responsible for all agreed-upon measures?

969. To what degree can team members vigorously define the teams purpose in considerations with others who are not part of the functioning team?

970. Can familiarity breed backup?

971. How does Application Functionality project termination impact Application Functionality project team members?

3.9 Team Member Performance Assessment: Application Functionality

972. Does statute or regulation require the job responsibility?

973. To what degree is the team cognizant of small wins to be celebrated along the way?

974. What does collaboration look like?

975. To what degree do team members frequently explore the teams purpose and its implications?

976. What are the evaluation strategies (e.g., reaction, learning, behavior, results) used. What evaluation results did you have?

977. How do you work together to improve teaching and learning?

978. To what degree are the goals ambitious?

979. What are the key duties or tasks of the Ratee?

980. What future plans (e.g., modifications) do you have for your program?

981. What is the large, desired outcome?

982. How do you currently use the time that is available?

983. What steps have you taken to improve performance?

984. How are assessments designed, delivered, and otherwise used to maximize training?

985. How does your team work together?

986. What happens if a team member receives a Rating of Unsatisfactory?

987. Is it critical or vital to the job?

988. What is collaboration?

989. Why were corresponding selected?

990. What, if any, steps are available for employees who feel they have been unfairly or inaccurately rated?

991. To what degree does the team possess adequate membership to achieve its ends?

3.10 Issue Log: Application Functionality

992. Is it a change in scope?

993. In classifying stakeholders, which approach to do so are you using?

994. How do you reply to this question; you am new here and managing this major program. How do you suggest you build your network?

995. Do you feel a register helps?

996. Which team member will work with each stakeholder?

997. What approaches do you use?

998. Are there too many who have an interest in some aspect of your work?

999. Who were proponents/opponents?

1000. Who do you turn to if you have questions?

1001. Do you prepare stakeholder engagement plans?

1002. What help do you and your team need from the stakeholders?

1003. What is the status of the issue?

1004. Which stakeholders can influence others?

1005. What would have to change?

1006. What is a change?

1007. Are the stakeholders getting the information they need, are they consulted, are concerns addressed?

4.0 Monitoring and Controlling Process Group: Application Functionality

1008. What is the timeline?

1009. User: who wants the information and what are they interested in?

1010. What communication items need improvement?

1011. What factors are contributing to progress or delay in the achievement of products and results?

1012. Does the solution fit in with organizations technical architectural requirements?

1013. Who needs to be engaged upfront to ensure use of results?

1014. Is it what was agreed upon?

1015. Where is the Risk in the Application Functionality project?

1016. Are there areas that need improvement?

1017. What do they need to know about the Application Functionality project?

1018. What will you do to minimize the impact should a risk event occur?

1019. What resources are necessary?

1020. How should needs be met?

1021. Just how important is your work to the overall success of the Application Functionality project?

1022. Did it work?

1023. How is agile portfolio management done?

1024. Do clients benefit (change) from the services?

1025. What is the timeline for the Application Functionality project?

1026. How are you doing?

1027. How well defined and documented were the Application Functionality project management processes you chose to use?

4.1 Project Performance Report: Application Functionality

1028. What is the degree to which rules govern information exchange between groups?

1029. To what degree will the team adopt a concrete, clearly understood, and agreed-upon approach that will result in achievement of the teams goals?

1030. What is in it for you?

1031. To what degree does the teams work approach provide opportunity for members to engage in open interaction?

1032. To what degree does the formal organization make use of individual resources and meet individual needs?

1033. To what degree do team members feel that the purpose of the team is important, if not exciting?

1034. To what degree are fresh input and perspectives systematically caught and added (for example, through information and analysis, new members, and senior sponsors)?

1035. To what degree can the cognitive capacity of individuals accommodate the flow of information?

1036. To what degree do individual skills and abilities match task demands?

1037. To what degree does the funding match the requirement?

1038. To what degree are the teams goals and objectives clear, simple, and measurable?

1039. To what degree does the teams approach to its work allow for modification and improvement over time?

1040. To what degree are the members clear on what they are individually responsible for and what they are jointly responsible for?

1041. How can Application Functionality project sustainability be maintained?

1042. To what degree does the informal organization make use of individual resources and meet individual needs?

1043. To what degree do the relationships of the informal organization motivate taskrelevant behavior and facilitate task completion?

1044. To what degree is there centralized control of information sharing?

1045. How will procurement be coordinated with other Application Functionality project aspects, such as scheduling and performance reporting?

4.2 Variance Analysis: Application Functionality

1046. Budget versus actual. how does the monthly budget compare to actual experience?

1047. Did a new competitor enter the market?

1048. Are authorized changes being incorporated in a timely manner?

1049. Contract line items and end items?

1050. Is work progressively subdivided into detailed work packages as requirements are defined?

1051. Are there knowledgeable Application Functionality projections of future performance?

1052. What should management do?

1053. How are material, labor, and overhead variances calculated and recorded?

1054. Are there changes in the direct base to which overhead costs are allocated?

1055. Did an existing competitor change strategy?

1056. What does a favorable labor efficiency variance mean?

1057. How do you identify and isolate causes of

favorable and unfavorable cost and schedule variances?

1058. Are data elements reconcilable between internal summary reports and reports forwarded to the stakeholders?

1059. Does the scheduling system identify in a timely manner the status of work?

1060. How do you evaluate the impact of schedule changes, work around, et?

1061. Is the market likely to continue to grow at this rate next year?

1062. Are overhead costs budgets established on a basis consistent with the anticipated direct business base?

1063. Are overhead cost budgets established for each department which has authority to incur overhead costs?

1064. Are there externalities from having some customers, even if they are unprofitable in the short run?

1065. Do work packages consist of discrete tasks which are adequately described?

4.3 Earned Value Status: Application Functionality

1066. Where is evidence-based earned value in your organization reported?

1067. What is the unit of forecast value?

1068. If earned value management (EVM) is so good in determining the true status of a Application Functionality project and Application Functionality project its completion, why is it that hardly any one uses it in information systems related Application Functionality projects?

1069. Validation is a process of ensuring that the developed system will actually achieve the stakeholders desired outcomes; Are you building the right product? What do you validate?

1070. Verification is a process of ensuring that the developed system satisfies the stakeholders agreements and specifications; Are you building the product right? What do you verify?

1071. How does this compare with other Application Functionality projects?

1072. When is it going to finish?

1073. Earned value can be used in almost any Application Functionality project situation and in almost any Application Functionality project environment. it may be used on large Application Functionality projects, medium sized Application Functionality projects, tiny Application Functionality projects (in cut-down form), complex and simple Application Functionality projects and in any market sector. some people, of course, know all about earned value, they have used it for years - but perhaps not as effectively as they could have?

1074. Where are your problem areas?

1075. How much is it going to cost by the finish?

1076. Are you hitting your Application Functionality projects targets?

4.4 Risk Audit: Application Functionality

1077. How do you govern assets?

1078. What are the differences and similarities between strategic and operational risks in your organization?

1079. Do you have a mechanism for managing change?

1080. Do you promote education and training opportunities?

1081. Are duties out-of-class?

1082. Do staff understand the extent of duty of care?

1083. Are all managers or operators of the facility or equipment competent or qualified?

1084. Have you reviewed your constitution within the last twelve months?

1085. Do you have position descriptions for all office bearers/staff?

1086. What does internal control mean in the context of the audit process?

1087. Are tools for analysis and design available?

1088. Are procedures in place to ensure the security of staff and information and compliance with privacy legislation if applicable?

1089. What are the boundaries of the auditors responsibility for policing management fidelity?

1090. What are the legal implications of not identifying a complete universe of business risks?

1091. Estimated size of product in number of programs, files, transactions?

1092. Is the number of people on the Application Functionality project team adequate to do the job?

1093. Does willful intent modify risk-based auditing?

1094. Is the technology to be built new to your organization?

4.5 Contractor Status Report: Application Functionality

1095. If applicable; describe your standard schedule for new software version releases. Are new software version releases included in the standard maintenance plan?

1096. What are the minimum and optimal bandwidth requirements for the proposed solution?

1097. What was the final actual cost?

1098. Describe how often regular updates are made to the proposed solution. Are corresponding regular updates included in the standard maintenance plan?

1099. What was the actual budget or estimated cost for your organizations services?

1100. Are there contractual transfer concerns?

1101. How is risk transferred?

1102. What was the overall budget or estimated cost?

1103. What was the budget or estimated cost for your organizations services?

1104. How long have you been using the services?

1105. What is the average response time for answering a support call?

1106. What process manages the contracts?

1107. How does the proposed individual meet each requirement?

1108. Who can list a Application Functionality project as organization experience, your organization or a previous employee of your organization?

4.6 Formal Acceptance: Application Functionality

1109. General estimate of the costs and times to complete the Application Functionality project?

1110. What lessons were learned about your Application Functionality project management methodology?

1111. How well did the team follow the methodology?

1112. Did the Application Functionality project achieve its MOV?

1113. Was the sponsor/customer satisfied?

1114. Was the Application Functionality project managed well?

1115. What are the requirements against which to test, Who will execute?

1116. How does your team plan to obtain formal acceptance on your Application Functionality project?

1117. Who supplies data?

1118. What features, practices, and processes proved to be strengths or weaknesses?

1119. What is the Acceptance Management Process?

1120. What function(s) does it fill or meet?

1121. Was the client satisfied with the Application Functionality project results?

1122. Does it do what Application Functionality project team said it would?

1123. Was the Application Functionality project work done on time, within budget, and according to specification?

1124. Is formal acceptance of the Application Functionality project product documented and distributed?

1125. Do you perform formal acceptance or burn-in tests?

1126. Does it do what client said it would?

1127. Who would use it?

1128. Was the Application Functionality project goal achieved?

5.0 Closing Process Group: Application Functionality

1129. What is the Application Functionality project Management Process?

1130. Is this a follow-on to a previous Application Functionality project?

1131. Specific - is the objective clear in terms of what, how, when, and where the situation will be changed?

1132. Is this an updated Application Functionality project Proposal Document?

1133. Did you do what you said you were going to do?

1134. What can you do better next time, and what specific actions can you take to improve?

1135. What were the desired outcomes?

1136. Just how important is your work to the overall success of the Application Functionality project?

1137. Is the Application Functionality project funded?

1138. How well did the chosen processes fit the needs of the Application Functionality project?

1139. Did the delivered product meet the specified requirements and goals of the Application Functionality project?

1140. Were the outcomes different from the already stated planned?

1141. Based on your Application Functionality project communication management plan, what worked well?

1142. What do you need to do?

1143. How well did you do?

1144. What is the risk of failure to your organization?

1145. What is an Encumbrance?

1146. What could have been improved?

5.1 Procurement Audit: Application Functionality

1147. Who had not previously applied to participate?

1148. Are regulations on taxes, fees, duties, excises, tariffs etc. not impeding (international) competition?

1149. Is there no evidence of false certifications?

1150. Has a deputy treasurer been appointed to sign checks when the treasurer is unable to perform that duty?

1151. Is the departments procurement function/unit well organized?

1152. Were the tender documents comprehensive, transparent and free from restrictions or conditions which would discriminate against certain suppliers?

1153. Are order quantities, deliveries and payment levels under the contract monitored by an appropriate official?

1154. Were exclusion causes duly considered before the actual evaluation of tenders?

1155. Are purchase orders pre-numbered?

1156. Are information gathered to produce knowledge about procured goods and services, prices paid and supplier performance?

1157. Are all mutilated and voided checks retained for proper accounting of pre-numbered checks?

1158. Has alternatives been considered for the specified procurement Application Functionality project?

1159. Are all initial purchase contracts made by the purchasing organization?

1160. Are outsourcing and Public Private Partnerships considered as alternatives to in-house work?

1161. Do you learn from benchmarking your own practices with international standards?

1162. Is authorization required to make changes to the purchase order file?

1163. Did the bidder comply with requests within the deadline set?

1164. Was the estimated contract value based on realistic and updated prices?

1165. Are there procedures to ensure that changes to purchase orders will be updated on the computer files?

1166. Does the cash disbursement policy prohibit drawing checks to cash or bearer?

5.2 Contract Close-Out: Application Functionality

1167. Was the contract complete without requiring numerous changes and revisions?

1168. Was the contract type appropriate?

1169. Parties: Authorized?

1170. Have all contract records been included in the Application Functionality project archives?

1171. Are the signers the authorized officials?

1172. Have all contracts been completed?

1173. How does it work?

1174. Why Outsource?

1175. How/when used ?

1176. How is the contracting office notified of the automatic contract close-out?

1177. Was the contract sufficiently clear so as not to result in numerous disputes and misunderstandings?

1178. Change in circumstances?

1179. Have all acceptance criteria been met prior to final payment to contractors?

1180. Parties: who is involved?

1181. Has each contract been audited to verify acceptance and delivery?

1182. What happens to the recipient of services?

1183. Have all contracts been closed?

1184. Change in knowledge?

1185. What is capture management?

1186. Change in attitude or behavior?

5.3 Project or Phase Close-Out: Application Functionality

1187. Does the lesson describe a function that would be done differently the next time?

1188. What was learned?

1189. When and how were information needs best met?

1190. Complete yes or no?

1191. What were the goals and objectives of the communications strategy for the Application Functionality project?

1192. What benefits or impacts does the stakeholder group expect to obtain as a result of the Application Functionality project?

1193. Is the lesson significant, valid, and applicable?

1194. Did the delivered product meet the specified requirements and goals of the Application Functionality project?

1195. Who controlled the resources for the Application Functionality project?

1196. How much influence did the stakeholder have over others?

1197. Which changes might a stakeholder be required to make as a result of the Application Functionality project?

1198. What hierarchical authority does the stakeholder have in your organization?

1199. Were risks identified and mitigated?

1200. How often did each stakeholder need an update?

1201. What is a Risk Management Process?

1202. What is the information level of detail required for each stakeholder?

1203. What are the mandatory communication needs for each stakeholder?

1204. Planned remaining costs?

5.4 Lessons Learned: Application Functionality

1205. Can the lesson learned be replicated?

1206. How much of your time was spent on other than this Application Functionality project?

1207. Were the right people available when required?

1208. Was the change control process properly implemented to manage changes to cost, scope, schedule, or quality?

1209. For the next Application Functionality project, how could you improve on the way Application Functionality project was conducted?

1210. What is the growth stage of your organization?

1211. Did the team work well together?

1212. What was the methodology behind successful learning experiences, and how might they be applied to the broader challenge of your organizations knowledge management?

1213. How comprehensive was integration testing?

1214. Did the Application Functionality project change significantly?

1215. How well do you feel the executives supported

this Application Functionality project?

1216. What needs to be done over or differently?

1217. What is the frequency of group communications?

1218. How clearly defined were the objectives for this Application Functionality project?

1219. Were any strategies or activities unsuccessful?

1220. How spontaneous are the communications?

1221. How actively and meaningfully were stakeholders involved in the Application Functionality project?

1222. How many government and contractor personnel are authorized for the Application Functionality project?

Index

staffed 33

Staffing 95, 193

standard 8, 93, 96, 129, 165, 247

standards 1, 10-11, 93, 98, 100, 129, 155, 186-187, 193, 211-212, 221, 254

started 9

starting 10, 136

start-up 133, 228

stated 111, 124, 184, 189, 252

statement 3, 11, 78, 83, 140, 147, 149

statements 12, 27, 32, 37, 43, 58, 66, 74, 90, 102, 126

static 220

status 5-6, 70, 156, 169, 175, 189-190, 193-194, 217, 228, 235, 242-243, 247

statute 233

statutory 227

steady 55

steering 150, 194

stopper 144

stories 42

strategic 46, 84, 97, 114, 130, 155, 211, 245

strategies 77, 95, 117, 123, 223-224, 226, 233, 260

strategy 26, 36, 45, 56, 79, 82, 100, 114, 119, 149, 199, 208, 224, 241, 257

Stream 69-70

strengths 149, 249

stretch 120

strict 64

strive 120

striving 130

Strongly 11, 16, 28, 44, 59, 75, 91, 104

structure 3-4, 110, 125, 151, 153, 167, 176, 209, 226

Structured 107

stubborn 104

stupid 115

subdivided 241

subject 9-10, 36

Subjective 186

subjects 66

submit 220

submitted 221-222

submitting 185

subset 25